D0089440

"Through heartfelt stories and mouthwatering recipes, Friedrich takes us on an intimate journey across Canada in order to remind us of the importance food plays in shaping our identities. *Your Canadian Food Story* is the conversation we ought to be having about food and a great reminder of what nourishment truly means."

Myriam Porrazzo, founder of *Mumspiration Food*

"*Your Canadian Food Story* is both a joy to read and an invaluable document. Not only does it capture the specific food stories of those living in Canada, but it also points out the universality of food and the experiences surrounding it. These stories (and the "Table Talk" questions accompanying them) beautifully highlight the resilience of Canadians when it comes to food, as well as the joy it imparts through so much more than just flavour."

Lindsay Anderson & Dana VanVeller, authors of *FEAST: Recipes & Stories from a Canadian Road Trip* (edibleroadtrip.com)

"*Your Canadian Food Story* was an absolute joy to revel in! After reading through the narratives of the storytellers and their love for food tied in with culture and community, I was reminded of my own unique food story. Loretta has thoughtfully curated a beautiful collection of heartwarming stories with delicious (and some quirky!) recipes, naturally encouraging readers to go down their own memory lane and be inspired to make something 'old' or new in the kitchen!"

Christal Sczebel, founder of *Nutrition in the Kitch* (nutritioninthekitch.com)

Your
Canadian
Food Story

Nourishing Stories and Recipes
from Across Canada

Dear Laura,
Thank you so much for your
support & interest in my project;
what's your food story?

xo
Loretta

LORETTA FRIEDRICH

Sprout Natural Nutrition
SproutNaturalNutrition.com

ISBN: 978-1-7752482-0-0

The information contained in this book is for self-education purposes
only and is not intended to provide specific advice to any individual. The
author or publisher cannot accept any responsibility for any ill effects
resulting from the use of the information and/or recipes found within
this book.

Stories and recipes used with permission.

Editing: Martin Friedrich
Editing, layout and design: Loretta Friedrich
Design: Emily Friedrich
Cover design: Dianna Bowes, fabulousat50.com
Front cover photo: RBOZUK, istockphoto.com
Interior image: AVIcons, istockphoto.com
Author photo: Bonnie-Jean McAllister, ealantaphotography.com
Back cover photo: Dianna Bowes & Loretta Friedrich

For information
about special discounts for bulk purchase
please contact the publisher:
SproutNaturalNutrition.com

First Edition

For

Martin

Emily

Laura

And all the people mentioned
in this food storybook.

CONTENTS

INTRODUCTION

Your Canadian Food Story is an invitation to come to the table to share our food stories and our knowledge about food, celebrate the uniqueness and value of every story, and pass the legacies of our stories to our children and grandchildren.

Food and food stories are a vital part of our culture, traditions, families, and communities. They comfort us when we're weary, help us celebrate our achievements, and create powerful legacies that enrich future generations. Food marks the routines of our days and the transitions and transformations of life; and by telling stories about food, we honour ourselves and our journeys. In all of these ways, food and food stories nourish us.

> **Nourish** (verb)
> 1. To sustain with food or nutriment; supply with what is necessary for life, health, and growth.
> 2. To cherish, foster, keep alive.
> 3. To strengthen, build up, or promote.
>
> **Nourishing** (adjective)
> 1. Promoting or sustaining life, growth, or strength.
>
> Source: Dictionary.com

Everyone has a food story because everyone has memories related to food. Whether conscious or not, these memories affect the way you view food. Both pleasant and painful memories are valuable because they are a part of who you are. By revealing and expressing your memories, and allowing them to speak to you, you can begin to tell your food story.

Many of us have experienced shame in relation to food, or been exposed to diets and fads that have left us empty or locked in food prisons. We can so easily lose our real stories in the constant pressures dictating what and how much we must eat; but we're released when we recognize the power of honouring our unique food stories. By telling and valuing your own food story, and by listening to and valuing the food stories of others, you can experience a freedom that perhaps you've never had before.

Why is your food story important? The answers to this question are the point of this book. It was written to:
- Celebrate food and its life-giving properties
- Honour and support food inheritance
- Share what we eat
- Acknowledge the value of food stories
- Keep food traditions and culture alive
- Pass down food legacy
- Feed food knowledge
- Nurture physical, emotional, mental, and spiritual health

This book evolved from my program *Your Food Story*, which is part of a larger mission to emphasize the importance of food stories and their whole health benefits. *Your Food Story* asks: Why do you eat, what, when, where, how and with whom? Where do you feel nourished? Does the food you eat affect your vitality? When do you feel satisfied with what you eat? Do you prefer eating with a group of people or alone? Etc. In other words, it's not just what we eat that gives us nourishment.

Read this book to:
- Connect with people from across Canada
- Discover patterns or similarities between stories
- Learn about regional foods
- Tap into the power of community
- Learn how to cook a special recipe
- Get creative in the kitchen
- Gather at the table and spark conversation
- Remember loved ones
- Nourish whole health

When you read some of the stories that follow you may wonder how certain foods could be thought of as nourishing. I suggest that whatever we eat can be nourishing, if we consider nourishment to be related to more than just eating the food itself. When I speak about food it's always in a holistic sense. We can be nourished in so many ways. I invite you to look at how the stories and recipes in this book are nourishing – not just in terms of caloric counting or what is considered "healthy," but also in terms of the nourishment we get from community, family, tradition, and all the other good things in life so intimately connected with food.

While this book focuses on food stories from all regions of Canada and salutes the Canadians who are in them, my desire is that no matter where you live, you would allow your own unique experiences and those recounted in this collection to boost your wellbeing. To get the most out of this book, I encourage you to feel the love or pain expressed in the stories, embrace the experience of eating and telling stories about food, relive your own memories, recognize your food history, and incorporate new customs in your daily life. In doing so, you will be nourished.

The Canadian Food Story

We acknowledge that Canada is much older than the act of confederation in 1867, and that our roots are planted on sacred treaty and aboriginal lands. First and foremost, we honour and respect the first peoples and their food legacy. We also honour and respect the immigrants who chose to make this great land their home, bringing with them food from all over the world. It is in the hope of reconciliation that we celebrate the beautiful diversity of Canadian food stories as well as the wonderful similarities between them that bind us all together.

Contributors

I made a very conscious effort to include contributors from all regions of Canada and often when I thought my efforts weren't enough, people would come forward from all over the country to offer their stories.

All 113 contributors represent not only our country's regional and cultural diversity but also our increasing mobility. While they are all Canadian-born or have immigrated to Canada, they may not currently reside in Canada. As well, the given locations of contributors are related to the stories they tell, even though they may no longer live there.

Each contributor has generously shared a personal experience about food that gives us an intimate glimpse into their lives and what food means to them. They have shared stories from their heart so that we can learn from them, be nourished, and be encouraged to share a food story as a result.

At the back of this book you'll find a list of contributors from each province or territory and the pages on which their stories appear. To learn more about each contributor, go to urfoodstory.com. Expect to find the passions, projects, or professions of contributors as well as pictures and links to websites, if applicable.

I am grateful to the people whose stories are in this book, and consider these wonderful folks now a part of my family. They have added richness to my own food story as I "sat at the table" with them. There's more room at the table; you are welcome to join our food community as well! Visit urfoodstory.com for more information and to learn how you can become involved.

Stories

Great care was taken to ensure that the contributor's voice was retained in each story, whether I interviewed them and wrote their story based on the notes I took when we met, or the contributor gave me a good starting point and then we penned the story together. If a contributor submitted a complete story, as editors we sometimes revised grammar and spelling but left the content as is for the most part. The goal was to invite you to meet each person as if you are listening to them share their story in person.

Several stories are about the same kind of food or dish. These stories were intentionally included to point out how each of our food stories is unique, even if we are talking about the same food. Everyone has a distinct and important food story to tell.

Recipes

Please be aware that the recipes have not been kitchen-tested except by the actual contributor. You'll see that most of the recipes provide (Imperial) measurements and can actually be used to create something to eat, whereas other recipes include only bundled food items (without measurements) that simply give us a picture of what has been referred to in the story.

While most contributors share a recipe, this book is not a cookbook per se. The recipes are there as supplements to the stories, which are the real heart of the book, not the other way around.

I encourage you to have fun – invite family or friends to create dishes with you as you follow the recipes. If you like, infuse your own taste preferences to create your own spin on a recipe. The recipe doesn't *have to* stay the same. In fact, you may not have some of the recipe's ingredients anyway due to availability. Who knows? You may very well begin a new tradition using one of the recipes. After all, it's your own food story you're creating!

Organization

While I did my best to fairly represent each region of Canada, the idea was not to draw attention to the actual number of stories from each area of the country. I intentionally chose not to group the stories by province or territory. Instead, since the overall theme of this book is about nourishment, the content is divided according to how we can be nourished by our stories, recipes or meals, within a Canadian context.

Food stories and recipes nourish:	
TRADITION	COMFORT
CULTURE	LIFE
FAMILY	CELEBRATION
COMMUNITY	LEGACY

These aspects of nourishment are fluid and blend into one another; for example, just because a story is in the "Family" chapter doesn't mean it couldn't also be relevant in the "Celebration" or "Tradition" chapters. Each story can be nourishing in many ways. My hope is that you read to answer questions like why, where, how, when, what food is being eaten and with whom, and how the story nourishes you.

Each chapter will have a brief introduction to the stories and recipes in that chapter, and conclude with a page called "Table Talk" that offers questions to answer if you so choose.

Please enjoy the stories from front to back, back to front, or dive into the book at any point; it is up to you how you read *Your Canadian Food Story*.

TRADITION

Tradition keeps us anchored and tethered. It offers stability and security in an uncertain world. There is a rich satisfaction that comes from knowing what to expect on certain occasions, anticipating these events, and sharing them with loved ones.

Food of course is an integral part of our traditions, since these traditions often involve the kinds of food we eat, with whom and when. Traditional food events are rooted in the occasion itself, but also perhaps in the preparation for the occasion as well as the post-event time spent with friends and family.

Like tradition, rituals can also sustain and enrich the rhythm of your life. A recurring food event, such as returning to the same berry patch every year, may not be a tradition in the same sense as the events surrounding a recurring shared meal; but rituals like berry picking or enjoying tea at a certain time of the day can be infused with the same sense of satisfaction and meaning as a food tradition.

Stories about tradition and personal rituals related to food are more about the events themselves than the handing down of traditions from generation to generation. This practice of passing down our traditions is so important that there is a separate chapter in this book dedicated solely to it, called "Legacy."

CHRISTINE HENNES
Laporte, Saskatchewan

One of the most significant rites of passage in Saskatchewan occurs once you reach the ripe old age of 12. This marks the time when you get your hunting license and are able to go on your first hunt.

My son Justin, now in his twenties, still looks forward to hunting birds each fall and comes out from the city to spend time hunting with his Dad. They head out in the early hours of the morning while the girls are still tucked under their covers in their toasty warm beds. The guys are up before sunrise to get all the decoys set in the field in just the perfect pattern, and then they watch the sunrise while waiting for the birds to land. Watching the birds setting their wings and gliding in amongst their decoys is a special thrill for these Saskatchewan hunters. One time they got a good laugh as a Canada Goose Justin shot misjudged the landing and smacked right into Justin's back. This was one of the more memorable moments they have had hunting, and they still talk about rude awakenings for the goose and Justin both.

Once the hunt is over, the work begins as the meat is taken off the birds in preparation for sausage making. As a family we have made sausage for many years and have refined our recipe to the one below. It is a yearly family project which provides us with tasty meat all winter long.

HENNES' HOMEMADE SAUSAGE

- 10 lbs goose and duck meat
- 32 lbs deer meat
- 20 lbs pork meat
- 16 lbs beef meat
- 1 ½ cups salt
- ¾ cup black pepper
- 1 ½ bulbs garlic
- 100 ml hot sauce (we use Firestick from Jamaica)
- 8 tsp apple liquid smoke
- 62 gms red pepper seasoning
- 2 oz curing salt

Grind all the meat and place in plastic bags after each hunt. Grate the garlic, place in a small piece of cheesecloth and tie the top, and then place into a bowl of water. Let stand for about 10 minutes.

Add all of the seasonings and the garlic juice to the ground meat. Then mix well in a large old washtub (ours has been in the family many generations). To test that the flavours are just right we make little patties and fry them up.

Once all the seasonings are well mixed we run the meat through the sausage stuffer and tie the sausage in meal-sized lengths for the extended family to enjoy throughout the winter.

PAULINE MAURIER
Edmonton, Alberta

We were a family of six kids, raised on the farm in the little community of Girouxville, Alberta. There were hard times, cold winters and crops to harvest. Occasionally, my parents struggled to ensure we always had a hot meal on the table. Dessert was a luxury item.

When my Mother had nothing to work with she'd get creative. She'd magically come up with something. Homemade bread lathered in thick farm cream and brown sugar... yum! (You should try it sometime.) I remember many occasions where we would indulge in sugar pie. Mom always had a big garden, so fresh raspberries and strawberries were always plentiful.

In the summer months we'd all get excited about packing a picnic lunch and venturing out into the country to pick wild berries. We were blessed with slews of blueberries, Saskatoons, cranberries and those teeny tiny little wild strawberries. Painstakingly hard to pick, but so worth the effort. Mom transformed them into her famous freezer jam. There's nothing like little wild strawberry freezer jam on homemade bread when it's 40 below outside.

But there's one true delicacy that was at the top of our list of favorites. La Tire! This was the REAL maple syrup home brew that was simmered on the wood stove to perfection, then poured onto clean white snow collected into a big dish from the yard. As Mom poured the hot maple syrup onto the snow it would get hard and sticky. With our forks in hand we would roll and twist La Tire till our forks were loaded. The combination of hot, cold and sweet is a childhood memory I will never forget.

Now, La Tire is a family tradition I introduced to my kids and my grandkids and hopefully many generations to come.

LA TIRE – MAPLE SYRUP ON THE SNOW

- **2 cups REAL maple syrup, to feed 8 people**
- clean snow ☺

Slowly boil the maple syrup on the stove until it's a good thick consistency. Test the readiness of the syrup by spooning up a small amount of syrup and letting it fall slowly from the spoon back into the pot. It should be like thick threads as it falls. Once this happens, you're ready.

Go outdoors and collect some clean white snow in a very large mixing bowl or trough. Slowly pour rows of maple syrup into the snow in long ribbons. It will harden as it cools on the snow. Then grab a fork and begin rolling and twisting the maple syrup onto your fork. Eat as you would a lollypop. Replenish snow and maple syrup as needed.

This is a very rich treat. Quantity is based on approximately ¼ cup of maple syrup per person. Example: 2 cups of maple syrup will feed 8 people. Add a ¼ cup for each additional person.

KATHY BLAKE
White Rock, British Columbia

There's nothing like opening up a can of sunshine deep in the heart of winter; but it all first begins during peak BC fruit season many months before, in either my kitchen or my girlfriend's, in what has become an annual tradition for over 25 years now.

You would be able to see that we take this canning day very seriously. People can't believe the massive amount of pears and peaches we purchase to capture the summer fruit deliciousness. In spite of the messy kitchen with syrup stains a-plenty, we enjoy visiting and catching up while steaming, peeling, cutting, sorting, stuffing, and bathing the fruit. At the end of the day, we are proud of the dozens of jars that will bring us and many others joy in the months to come.

We hand out these canned goods as a gift of love; everyone enjoys these bowls of happiness. The smiles on the faces of the hostess or those who are sick or shut-in verifies the reason to continue to do as our ancestors did – though they did not have the modern canners or stoves like we do – and preserve food to enjoy later. My kids were especially grateful for these treats in their care package while away living in residence at university. They couldn't wait to taste home in every spoonful.

Canned fruit, with my favorite being pears, has been a staple food for many generations, and I hope for many generations to come. Consider giving canned peaches or pears and watch the grins appear.

CANNED PEARS

- pears – must be ripe
- sugar
- canning jars
- canning lids
- canning rings
- canner
- a good friend to visit with

Prepare the syrup by simply boiling the water and sugar until sugar dissolves using 2 cups sugar to 4 cups water.

Sterilize the jars – dishwasher is fine for the jars and rings. Place caps in a bowl of boiling water. Fill canner with water and bring it to a boil.

Peel and slice pears in quarters, remove core and seeds, and cut out any brown spots. Fill jars with pears, add the sugar water, and remove any air bubbles by running a knife between pears and jar.

Seal jars with cap and ring. Place sealed jars in canner and keep them covered with 1 inch of water. Boil in canner for 20 minutes.

JULIE BANKE-VILLENEUVE
Quebec City, Quebec

A Canadian French Catholic tradition is that family is not allowed to eat the Christmas meal until after attending midnight mass, which would be around 1:30am. The aroma of tourtière would welcome our taste buds when we got back from church.

Preparing for this annual meal actually started months in advance with the making of tourtière. Mon papa was in charge of the meat filling. He was the expert. Ma grand-maman looked after the pastry. And my mom? Well, we all recognized that she did not have strong cooking skills so we did not encourage her to help in any way! She would offer comments, but when she noticed nobody was paying attention she would pour herself a generous glass of red wine. And again. You see a trend going on. The worst was to have to wait until Christmas to eat the pie knowing that in the meantime they were wrapped up in the freezer for many weeks! Often I would ask to have tourtiere for dinner, but NO, we were not allowed before Christmas.

When it was finally time to eat the delicious tourtière – as the main part of the meal – we enjoyed it with a lot of people; there were typically at least 40 people at my parent's place! Then under the guidance of a cousin or aunt, with a bottle of ketchup in hand, we'd decorate each piece of pie with whatever designs came to mind. It had to be ketchup. Mustard was forbidden and looked upon as being weird!

To this day, this meal reminds me of Christmas tradition, even more special now since my mom, dad, and grandmother have passed. I have siblings to hold and hopefully keep the tradition alive.

TOURTIÈRE

Pastry

- 2 ½ cups flour
- ½ cup unsalted butter
- 2 Tbsp lemon juice
- ½ tsp fine salt
- ½ cup shortening
- 6 to 10 Tbsp cold water

Combine flour with salt. Cut in butter and shortening until a crumbly texture. Add lemon juice and water. Blend just until dough comes together. Shape into disc. Wrap. Chill 30 minutes. Prepare filling.

Filling

- 1 ½ cup diced, potatoes
- 1 ½ lbs ground pork, veal, and/or beef
- 2 onions, diced
- 2 clove garlic, minced
- 2 bay leaves
- ¾ tsp fine salt
- ¼ tsp gr. black pepper
- ½ tsp crushed celery seed
- dash each allspice and ground cloves
- 1 cup apple cider
- ½ cup water
- 1 egg + 2 Tbsp water

Cook potatoes in water until tender. Drain. Roughly mash potatoes. Set aside. In large pan, sauté meat over medium heat until no longer pink. Drain fat. Add onions, garlic and seasonings. Sauté until tender, about 10 minutes. Add cider and water. Simmer for about 15 minutes until most of liquid is absorbed. Remove from heat, stir in potatoes. Cool to room temperature. This can be prepared a day in advance.

Preheat oven to 375 °F. On a floured surface, cut dough in half, roll out to about ¼-inch thickness and line an 8-inch spring form pan. Fill with tourtière filling. Roll out remaining dough, cut a hole in center (for steam to escape). Place on top of filling. Pinch edges of crust together. Mix egg with water (to make egg wash). Brush crust with egg wash. Bake for 40 to 45 minutes, until pastry is a golden brown. Let cool 5 minutes. Remove from pan and serve.

Note: Tourtière can be made in advance and frozen. Then defrost in the fridge overnight and reheat in a 350 °F oven for 45 minutes or until a knife is inserted and is hot in the middle of the blade

JANET HAUSER
Prince Albert, Saskatchewan

From my earliest memories, my family celebrated Christmas Eve by having fondue together. My father, a true carnivore at heart, would rub his hands, lick his lips and search for that perfect piece of tenderloin to immerse in the hot oil and cook to perfection, dip in a favorite sauce, and enjoy!

We are not Swiss or French, but Swedish by ethnicity on my father's side and chose to celebrate with a special meal on Christmas Eve as the Swedes do.

As children, we would run around the house that day dancing with glee that we were going to have "fun-due" that night! It always seemed magical to me, the hot oil, the shrimp, steak and mushrooms, real grown up food, the special sauces, taking time over the meal as it cooked, and being able to cook my own food on a fancy fork! We just had to remember which colour our forks were. And, if we lost an item in the oil, we were supposed to kiss someone at the table. My mom would have lots of candles lit around the house, and the Swedish chimes would be ringing out as we prepared to eat.

Canadian beef is truly wonderful! We enjoy the tender, flavorful meat. We've lived in other places around the world and still enjoy the Canadian beef tenderloin the very most!

This meal has become an enduring tradition as our family has grown and changed. All of us continue to follow it, though we live in various parts of North America. We are looking forward to the next generation to carry on with it as they establish their own families. Giving a fondue pot and equipment has become the Christmas gift for newlyweds.

CHRISTMAS EVE FONDUE

Purchase cooking oil. (My dad usually used peanut oil due to its high smoke temperature, but you can also use grapeseed or canola oil.) Make or buy garlic bread. Prepare a Caesar salad.

- beef tenderloin, cut into chunks
- shrimp (fresh or frozen), thaw, de-vein, dry on paper towels
- mushrooms, washed and dried
- If desired: chicken breast and/or pork, cut into chunks

Put meat, shrimp, and mushrooms in separate bowls and keep refrigerated until time to cook.

Cold White Sauce

- sour cream, to taste
- green onions, to taste
- mayonnaise, to taste

Cold Tomato Sauce

- ½ cup chili sauce
- 2 Tbsp honey
- 1 tsp soy sauce

Hot Steak

- 1/3 cup steak sauce (we use Heinz 57)
- 1 cup ketchup
- 2 Tbsp brown sugar
- 2 Tbsp canola oil

In separate bowls, for each cold sauce, combine ingredients well. Refrigerate until ready to serve. (Can be made a day in advance.)

For the hot steak sauce, in a saucepan, combine all ingredients. Stir and bring to a boil. Keep hot until ready to serve.

About 30 minutes before cooking time put cooking oil in pan and pre-heat on stove top.

When ready to eat, pour hot oil in fondue pot and place on the table with the sauces. Enjoy with salad and bread!

WENDY FOSTER
Stratford, Prince Edward Island

It's clam digging time! Mom, Grandma Cook, and Great Aunt Nan load up the back of our little Ford Pinto station wagon with large buckets, shovels, spades, and us kids. No seat belts, no worries… just time for fun at the beach on Prince Edward Island.

We help dig and quickly fill the buckets with the large bar clams that Mom will eventually make into our favourite treat – Uncle Tom's Clam Balls. Funny, 'cause it's not *our* Uncle Tom, just *an* Uncle Tom – such is the island way… and I can just hear Mom joking, "I betcha didn't even know them clams had balls!" I just love her P.E.I. accent!

All fun aside, a lot of work goes into this process once the buckets are full, covered in ocean water, and lugged home. After they are cooked, the nasty job of cleaning begins. I've done that one time too many, but Mom can practically do it with her eyes closed! Next, there's chopping and prepping for the freezer. It is a hard day's labour of love.

When company comes "from away," usually Ontario or Boston, Mom takes the clams out of the freezer, prepares her bowl of "goop," scoops it up by the spoonful, and gingerly places it into the hot oil. She is always drenched in sweat as she stands over the stove in the tiny, hot galley kitchen, but she never complains.

Mom has been making Clam Balls for over 60 years. Under her careful and expert watch, the lumps of goop seem to cook themselves and transform into delectable, fluffy golden brown balls. The feeding frenzy then begins! After everyone has their fill, Mom finally serves herself. The joy on her face is not from the food, but from the delight on the faces of her beloved guests. Thanks for the memories, Mom! I'll be home for Clam Balls this summer!

MOM'S (AND UNCLE TOM'S) CLAM BALLS

- 2 cups coarsely ground or chopped bar clams
- 2 cups flour
- 2 eggs
- 2 tsp baking powder
- "enough clam juice to make consistency of drop cookie batter"

Heat vegetable oil in a large pot. Mix all ingredients in a bowl. Scoop by the spoonful. Gently place in the oil. "Balls will turn over on their own like doughnuts." Cook until golden brown. Place on plate covered with paper towel to remove excess grease. Serve with ketchup, salt and pepper.

BARRY SIEMENS
Osler, Saskatchewan

Twenty eight years ago I met my wife Crystal Fehr, who was raised in a Mennonite background the same way as my dad. When I started dating her we took a trip to Osler, Saskatchewan, to her mom and dad's dairy farm. It was there that I was introduced to a food that has become my favorite ever since.

For supper my (future) mother-in-law made a soup called Grandma's Summer Borscht, which was her mom's soup she ate while growing up. It was so good that we now have it on a regular basis. It is a meal in itself because it very filling. It is prepared just like any other soup, from scratch. Not only does it smell good, it tastes so good that it will have you craving for more. The creamy dill broth is to die for!

This is a Mennonite (summer) tradition and has been carried on for generations. Here is the recipe...

GRANDMA'S SUMMER BORSCHT SOUP

- 8 to 10 large potatoes
- sausage or ham bone with meat
- large onion, diced
- dill, chopped
- wild sour leaves, chopped
- green onions, chopped
- 1 cup each sour cream and whipping cream or 2 cups buttermilk, to taste

Gather together dill, sour leaves, and onion greens. (If you can't find wild sour leaves you can use young beet leaves instead.) Store in plastic bags consider freezing in bags or jars for when you're ready to make the soup.

Cook a ham bone or sausage. Add pieces of the meat – you can put in as much meat as you like – and onion in a half a pot of water. Put the dill mix in a cheese cloth or spice container, place in pot, and simmer all for an hour.

In the meantime peel and cut potatoes into cubes, then add to the rest of the ingredients in the pot. We like a lot of potatoes in the soup but add however much you prefer.

When potatoes are done cooking, stir in the buttermilk or cream combination. Eat to your heart's content!

OLGA NYMAN

Toronto, Ontario

On special occasions across this great land of ours called Canada, wherever family, friends or groups gather to share a meal together, their traditional ethnic or favorite dishes are prepared, featured and displayed prominently with much fanfare on backyard picnic tables, buffet style tables and dining room tables. We are thankful for our land of plenty. Here's my story:

For the past 35 years, the Sweet Potato Pie has held first place on our family's festive table at each special occasion including all major celebratory holidays. The mouthwatering aroma and distinct sweet flavor enhances all the other fancy dishes gracing the "groaning boards" of familiar family favorites. This dish complements such a variety of meats: ham, lamb, turkey, beef, chicken, pork and salmon. Each diner awaits the dinner date with great anticipation.

Many years ago our young family enjoyed baked sweet potatoes in their jackets with butter and cinnamon at every day meals, until I discovered a new and improved way of preparing our family's staple. This dish was highly favored by young and old alike. Visiting guests and potluck supper people always requested my recipe. It's gratifying to know it is a much travelled dish, now having been served in several Canadian provinces, some American states and a few foreign lands.

My love of sweet potatoes began many years ago at my first tasting in California, where they were called yams and were served exotically with candied pears, apricots, prunes and pecans. I then introduced my young family to a new vegetable and they loved it! Now my grown children all serve our family dish at their homes and gatherings, while the very young ones are fed plain sweet potatoes mashed with cooked broccoli florettes and flaked baked salmon, minus the crunchy crust, butter and sugar.

SWEET POTATO PIE

Filling

- 6 large sweet potatoes
- 1 tsp salt
- ½ tsp pepper
- 1 stick butter
- ¼ cup brown sugar or maple syrup

Topping

- 1 stick butter
- ½ cup brown sugar, firmly packed
- 2 cups corn flakes, hand-crushed slightly

To make the filling, wash unpeeled sweet potatoes and dry off. Prick the potatoes in several places with a knife. Arrange them to fit into a glass 10 inch pie plate. Microwave 8 to 10 minutes. Turn each one. Microwave 5 to 10 minutes more (check for softness but do not overcook). Carefully remove. Cool 5 minutes.

Peel off potato skins, discard. Place soft contents in a mixing bowl. With a fork, mash the hot potatoes with the rest of the ingredients. Whip until very smooth. Wash the same pie plate, dry it off, and then add this filling, packing it down firmly.

To make the topping, in the microwave, melt butter. Remove. Add brown sugar, stir, mixing well as sugar dissolves in the hot butter. Add handfuls of crunched corn flakes into the butter/sugar mixture. Keep mixing while adding more crunched corn flakes until you have a full dish of the buttered cornflakes. Spread cornflake mixture evenly on top of the pressed sweet potatoes, making sure to cover completely.

In 350F oven, bake for 25 minutes until the pie is heated throughout and the topping (crust) is crunchy brown. Do not burn! Keep an eye on the crust near the end of cooking time.

Hint: Double this recipe to make two pies, as one usually is never enough. Reheating leftovers works well.

COLLEEN REMPEL
Morris, Manitoba

I have wonderful memories of helping my grandma in her garden when I was around seven years old. Picture a huge garden that takes up most of her backyard, filled with tons of fruits and vegetables. My favourite memory is helping her pick and wash raspberries from the giant raspberry patch. The raspberry bushes were taller than me and I felt like I was exploring a maze when I would sneak between the rows to pick the little ruby morsels.

I spent many weeks during the summer at Grandma's place in this little town about 30 minutes south of Winnipeg. It became part of my growing up years, and to this day, it's the tradition of harvesting raspberries that floods me with warm memories. Here I felt rooted and learned about my families farming background; I really bonded with my dad's mom during this special time.

While I live in Winnipeg now, the emotional ties are still strong. My grandmother is well into her 80s, but if I can't make it back in time for picking, she usually finds a way to send along berries with someone to ensure I have some fresh ones to enjoy. Even if we don't get any fresh raspberries, the whole Rempel family can still count on Grandma to preserve some of them in her special raspberry jam, a German Mennonite tradition.

At every family gathering, this jam would be served a few hours after a meal, with homemade buns and butter. If I can't get her supply, I'll go to the local farmer's markets to enjoy some fresh raspberries, or I may make them into something like a raspberry chia seed jam or chia seed pudding.

Can you tell that raspberries are my favorite fruit?

GRANDMA REMPEL'S RASPBERRY JAM

- 4 cups prepared raspberries
- 8 cups organic cane sugar
- 4 Tbsp fresh lemon juice

- 2 fruit pectin packages (I use Certo®)
- 12-13 x 250ml glass mason jars

Rinse clean glass jars and lids with boiling water. Crush raspberries and remove seeds. Combine raspberries and sugar in a large bowl. Let stand for 10 mins, stirring a few times.

Mix pectin and lemon juice. Then add to bowl with raspberry/sugar mix. Stir mixture until all of the sugar is dissolved.

Fill all jars immediately, leaving ½ inch of space from the top. Wipe off top and sides of containers, and cover with lids right away.

Let stand at room temperature for 24 hours. Then the jam is ready to use. Store in fridge for 3 weeks or freeze for up to 1 year. Thaw frozen jam in refrigerator before using.

MARK FARTHING
Harrison Hot Springs, British Columbia

Blackberries grow all over the Fraser Valley. My method of picking is to drive near the Fraser River and stop when I see a bush or two. In addition, I ride into the backcountry, since they also grow in almost all the ditches there. If you come to an unkempt area the blackberries there usually have the most berries.

They can be easy to pick, but in some places it is almost impossible if you don't like getting stuck by the extremely long thorns. The thorns are shaped like hooks, so they easily catch on clothes, drawing you in; as you move to unhook you get hooked in more places. Typically, to get to the best berries you have to reach and twist your body. When you get poked it hurts so much you move quickly and get poked again! Before you know it you are tenderly extracting two or three spikes from yourself.

The berries are usually plentiful and I can get about four pounds in an hour, assuming that the bush has not been picked over. You will find the easier-to-reach bushes get picked very early in the season. If you want the best you have to be prepared for pain, but I have used the pain as a learning tool. I get hooked far less than when I started three years ago. To me, it is worth it because I enjoy eating them, specially made into a sauce. Much of the nutritional part of the seed of the whole berry is not absorbed by humans unless the seed is macerated. I use this sauce recipe to break down the berries and for all kinds of berries and other fruits too.

BERRY SAUCE FOR MEAT

- 1 colander of blackberries
- 2/3 cup of mixed lemon, lime, orange (I use one of each just because I like the acid level)
- ½ cup brown sugar
- ½ cup white sugar

Cook until boiling. Remove from heat and process through a food mill. Bottle in sterilized jars and lids.

I like to preserve where I have the most options down the road: use the sauce as is, thicken it later, or add something to it like chilies and the like. If I want it a bit thicker at the time of cooking, I add a couple of teaspoons of pectin. (Starch will degrade over time due to acid.) Pack in jars using the proper canning procedures.

Personally I use most of this sauce on meat, especially pork. I think meat and fruit go well together, as the fruit helps digest the meat.

REBECCA TWEIDT
Saskatoon, Saskatchewan

Perogies are by far one of the most popular dishes eaten by families in Saskatchewan. This cherished favorite is eaten at many events, including traditional Christmas dinners, fall suppers and all-you-can-eat perogies fundraisers. Known as "perogi" to our Ukrainian family, the little dumplings are an essential part of our Christmas dinner.

My extended family gathers in November to prepare the perogies that we will serve at Christmas. We all take part in the various tasks of preparing the perogies. The dough is prepared and rolled out onto the dining room table, where we cut circular pieces into the dough. My family makes a traditional stuffing of potatoes, cottage cheese, and spices, but there are many variations. We all sit around the table and begin to fold the dough over a ball of stuffing, pressing the edges so that it forms a semicircle-shaped dumpling. We layer them onto wax paper on baking sheets and put them in the freezer until Christmas. Each family takes home a few trays to put in their deep freeze, usually with a few extras to eat.

On Christmas Eve, we prepare the Ukrainian-style Christmas dinner with all of the other essential dishes: cabbage rolls, pickled herring, and baked fish. The perogies are prepared by boiling them in water for a few minutes. They are served with sautéed onions, melted butter, and sour cream.

While perogies are a favorite in my family and are served at all times of the year, the best influence that perogies have in my life is the Christmas tradition that my family and I share in and the joy we experience when connecting over food.

CHUBACK FAMILY'S UKRAINIAN PEROGIES

This recipe is in loving memory of Auntie Sophie.

Dough

- 10 cups flour
- 1 Tbsp salt
- 1 cup margarine
- 2 eggs
- 2 cups milk
- 2 cups cold water

Add flour, salt and margarine in a large bowl. Blend to a fine mealy consistency. In a separate bowl, blend eggs, milk and cold water. Add to dry mixture to form the dough. Let dough rest for 20 min to 1 hour.

Filling

- 3-5 large potatoes, cooked, mashed
- 1 cup cottage cheese
- 1 egg yolk (from a large egg)
- 1 Tbsp butter, melted
- ¼ tsp salt
- pinch of pepper, to taste

In a separate bowl, mix all the filling ingredients together to create the filling. Set aside.

Roll out dough on flat surface. Cut pieces out of dough using a glass. Put a spoonful of filling on a piece of dough and fold over filling. Press edges of dough to create a semicircle-shaped pocket with filling inside.

To freeze, dust with flour, place on wax paper on baking sheets, and place in freezer.

Bring a large pot of water to a boil. Drop fresh or frozen perogies into pot and cook for about 4 minutes or until they all float at the surface. (Frozen perogies may need to cook longer than fresh ones.)

Serve with sautéed onions, melted butter, and sour cream.

LORI GALLANT
Paradise, Newfoundland and Labrador

Anyone familiar with the traditions in Newfoundland and Labrador knows that Jiggs dinner is served pretty much every Sunday. Growing up in my house – and many other homes in NL – Saturday was often soup day. It could be likely that soup was prepared on Saturdays because a heavy and hearty meal – like Jiggs dinner – was always eaten on Sundays. It also takes time to cook Jiggs dinner.

The type of soup varied, but a favourite in many homes was and still is pea soup with dumplings, aka "dough by's." (The salt beef/salt meat used in this soup is the main part in Sunday's meal, Jiggs dinner.) The thicker the pea soup the better, and on foggy days in Newfoundland you can hear people say "the fog is as thick as pea soup."

Who typically prepared the soup? My mother. Even to this day her pea soup is the best. Gathered around the table to enjoy the soup usually was my father, mother, sister and I, but often a friend or two would be there as well. I also remember my grandfather coming down to our house for some.

Although I love pea soup I do not make it nearly as often as my mother did. I do, however, prepare it maybe once a month, and my two little girls help. By the way, the pea soup tastes even better left over!

NEWFOUNDLAND PEA SOUP

- 3 to 3 ½ cups dried split peas
- 3 cups salt beef, cubed
- 1 ½ onion, chopped
- 4 liters water
- 1 large turnip, chopped
- 6 carrots, chopped

Cube salt beef, and soak overnight in water. Strain. Add beef and chopped onion to a pot filled with 4 liters water. Wash peas, strain, and add to pot. Bring to a boil and then turn heat down to low and simmer. When beef is tender, add turnip and carrots until cooked.

DOUGH BY'S/DUMPLINGS

- 2 cups of flour
- ½ tsp salt
- 3 heaping Tbsp baking powder
- 1 cup of cold water

Put flour in a bowl with salt and baking powder. Slowly add cold water and mix (do not beat) until "doughy." Drop dough in soup (about a Tbsp for each dumpling and not touching). Cover and let cook for 8-10 minutes. Dumplings are often used as a dessert as well. Take out of soup and put jam or molasses on them.

MARIE MACDONALD
Fort Smith, Northwest Territories

Although I was born in Northwest Territories, I was raised in Alberta. Growing up, I was very curious about my roots, since my father was a Northern First Nations man and my mother was an immigrant from England.

During an adventure in the N.W.T., I met my future husband and joined him after we married to live there. I had a lot to learn about Northern living, but one thing I embraced was the tradition of harvesting wild berries, especially my favorite, the mighty cranberry (both high and low bush varieties).

In September, the unmistakable scent of high bush berries is in the air. These bright red berries can easily be seen as my eyes scan the brush, and are picked at about waist height. They do take more work to process, though, as they have a huge seed in the middle. I make delicious cranberry jelly served as a spread on bread, over melted Brie cheese, or even with turkey dinner.

Once I get a whiff of those high bush cranberries, I know the low bush are also ready to harvest. These dark tiny berries – that are found low, barely off the ground – are expertly camouflaged under fallen brush and often protected by thorny rosebushes. Their beautiful fragrance is released when cooked, and they have a tart but delightful flavour.

NOBODY in the North, including me, tells anyone else where their secret and best berry picking patch is! I look forward to fall when I can get harvest cranberries and prepare one of our favorites, a simple cake with sauce, enjoyed by all who eat it.

CRANBERRY CAKE WITH SAUCE

- 3 cups flour
- 4 tsp baking powder
- ½ tsp salt
- 4 Tbsp butter
- 1 ½ cups sugar
- 2-3 tsp real vanilla (I use Mexican)
- 1 ½ cups milk
- 3-4 cups WILD cranberries

Mix flour, baking powder and salt in a bowl and set aside. Cream together the butter, sugar and vanilla. (It does not get fluffy like a regular cake batter.) Add the flour mixture to the creamed mixture with milk, beating until just mixed – do not over mix. Stir in wild cranberries. (If you use the large commercial cranberries you will need to chop them up a bit.)

Spread the batter in a greased 9 X 13 inch pan. Bake in a 400F oven for about 40-50 min until it is golden brown and the top springs back when lightly touched.

BUTTER SAUCE

You must serve the cake with sauce; the secret to this cake is in the sauce!

- ¾ cups butter
- 1 ½ cups sugar
- ¾ cup evaporated milk

Combine the sauce ingredients in a saucepan and bring to a boil over medium heat. Stir constantly with a whisk. Simmer for 2 minutes and remove from heat. Serve the sauce warm over the cake. Enjoy!

VAL B. MICHAUD
Gravelbourg, Saskatchewan

There was a girl, a prairie girl, who out of six girls described herself as the "boy in the family." That girl was me! I grew up surrounded by acres and acres of land that produced crops like lentils, peas, wheat, canola, and mustard. In full bloom the sea of yellow from both canola and mustard was truly breathtaking... and still is.

I remember dad allowing us to jump in and out of mounds of seeds in the back of his grain truck; but my favourite memory was sitting on top of the granary, perched, scanning the fields, gazing into the distance for hours until I realized I should really respond to the calls of my mom, "Where are you?" Those were carefree days that I will remember for the rest of my life.

When the weather permitted, I rode my bike to town to attend school or other activities; it was pleasant to inhale the clean prairie air and take in the surrounding scenery. Once I arrived back home I found my mom either tending to the garden or waiting in the kitchen for us with a snack. Our favorite? Pretzels with a mayo/mustard dip.

I am proud to be in in the mustard producing business here in Gravelbourg, and while we have access to many different flavours, one of my family favourites is still the very tasty mustard/mayo dip with pretzels. This snack is a tradition with my family; my children grew up eating it at my parents' and my home and I'm sure it will be passed along as a family tradition for generations to come. Hope you enjoy!

PRETZELS WITH MUSTARD DIP

- bag of pretzels

- ½ part prepared mustard with ½ part mayonnaise

Stir the mustard and mayonnaise well together. Chill. Serve with pretzels!

Table Talk

- What is one of your favorite traditions involving food?

- Who participates in this tradition?

- When did you last take part in this tradition?

- Where does this tradition take place?

- Why is this tradition so special to you?

- Is there a ritual or habit that you follow daily, weekly, monthly, yearly or on occasion?

- What is the significance of this ritual or habit?

- What tradition would you like passed on to future generations?

CULTURE

The foods we have adopted or adapted have been shaped by our past and present environments. Our culture – defined as the beliefs, values, practices, and material traits of the social, ethnic or religious groups to which we belong – influences our relationship with food in many important ways. For example, it determines how we view the power or importance of food, what is acceptable to consume, and what portion size is appropriate. Without being bound by your culture, though, you can choose whatever it is from your own or other cultures that is nourishing, practice it, and share it with others through stories and food.

Our multicultural society, so apparent in the food stories shared in this chapter, is a cause for celebration. While cultural differences may sometimes drive people apart, when food is involved, difference tends to bring people together. Who hasn't been pleasantly surprised by the taste of an ethic dish? And then perhaps drawn to learn more about that culture because of our love of its food?

Food stories about culture encourage us to find opportunities to nourish and honour our various cultural/traditional backgrounds by sharing them with others.

LORALEE WETTLAUFER

St. John's, Newfoundland and Labrador

We are Newfoundlanders by choice. We have no family ties to Newfoundland, but seven years ago we fulfilled our 20 year dream to live somewhere new by moving to St. John's/Mount Pearl, Newfoundland. We believed that to adopt a new home meant immersing ourselves in the culture, the people, and the food.

After a few short weeks we began to ready ourselves to welcome our first "Come from Away" guests. We wanted to share our new home so we went looking for the food to serve. Jiggs dinner, also known as boiled dinner or Sunday dinner, was the choice. It is still served in many Newfoundland homes as Sunday dinner. That meal at noon on a Sunday, sometimes after church, when the family gathers to share a meal, share their lives and prepare for the coming week, is a kept tradition.

Now I did not have generations of grandmothers to learn from so I began by interviewing those around me to see how they prepared this meal. It's a meal prepared in one pot, made from ingredients that can be grown here in our shallow topsoil and short growing season, and it touches back to life on the water. Salt meat, potatoes, turnip, carrots, cabbage and dried yellow peas boiled in one pot and served sometimes with roasted meat and gravy, if not with the "liquor" from the cooking pot.

So I gathered the wisdom of co-workers and friends and their Mothers and Grandmothers and I set out to serve my first Jiggs dinner. The meal was a great success and received the stamp of approval from mainlanders and Newfoundlanders alike. The following recipe was developed from multiple conversations.

JIGGS DINNER

- salt meat
- dried yellow split peas
- cabbage

- turnip
- carrots
- potatoes

Soak the salt meat in water overnight, then drain. Boil in fresh water for a few hours. Place the dry peas in a peas pudding bag and tie closed. Make sure it is not too tight (or it will be too dry) and not too loose (or it will be too runny). Boil with the meat for a minimum of 1 hour.

Meanwhile, cut cabbage, turnip, carrots and potatoes in large chunks. In 15 minute intervals, beginning with the cabbage, add vegetables to the hot water. Cook until potatoes are tender.

Scoop all items from the water into separate serving dishes. Remove the peas from the peas pudding bag and top with a dab of butter.

Meal can be served with roasted meat, dressing, and gravy, or with a pitcher of the liquor (reserved water from cooking).

MARY PINCHUK
Toronto, Ontario

My mom made holubtsi (Ukrainian for cabbage rolls) for years, even before I was born, so I can't recall when I first had them because they were prepared often. They actually were one of the few foods I ate since I was a very choosy eater.

Holubtsi, translated as "little pigeons" in Ukrainian, were the right combination of tastes for me. I liked the rice, onions, and a bit of bacon wrapped in tender cabbage leaves. Sometimes buckwheat was mixed in with the rice too. The tomato taste suited me well, with some sour cream on top. Along with various soups – chicken soup as my favorite – holubtsi became a staple in my diet.

If it didn't come fresh from our garden or our cold storage room in the basement, my mother would buy the cabbage for holubtsi from the market. Both my parents worked, and we observed Sundays as our day of rest, so Saturdays were when my mother did the market shopping and prepared Sunday meals. After Sunday church, my mother would heat the holubtsi she had prepared the day before.

As I became older I helped with the process and learned the art of rolling. It's all in the hands. You let your hands do the work and guide you, adjusting your technique as you went along, according to the size of the cabbage leaf you were working with, using both your eyes and hands to create how many servings were needed. I took that knowledge with me when I had a household of my own. But doesn't it always seem that there's nothing like how mom used to make it?

I wouldn't say my mom was an overly affectionate person, but we sure enjoyed her delicious food. This was how she showed us her love.

HOLUBTSI OR UKRAINIAN CABBAGE ROLLS

- 1 large cabbage
- 1 ½ pounds pearl or long grain rice (or buckwheat as well)
- 5 medium onions, peeled, diced
- ½ pound butter
- salt, pepper, to taste
- 1 ½ cups tomato juice or enough to cover cabbage rolls
- ½ pound bacon, diced, optional
- sour cream, to serve

Remove core of cabbage. Place entire cabbage in pot of boiling water to wilt leaves. Separate leaves and cut off hard rib. Reserve any thicker outer leaves to line pot. Cover finished cabbage rolls on the end.

Cut remaining large leaves into about 4 pieces and smaller leaves into about 3 pieces, depending on size of cabbage and how big or small you want to make cabbage rolls.

Cook rice (and buckwheat if using) according to package instructions. While rice is cooking, fry onions in butter. If using bacon, fry in another pan, drain, and add to rice and onions.

Place a cabbage leaf in palm of one hand and then place approximately 1 Tbsp on the leaf. With help from the other hand, roll up slightly and tuck ends as you go along so rice does not show, to keep roll intact.

If using a large pot, place a tall glass in the middle before lining up cabbage rolls in neat rows. Then when pot is full, remove glass before pouring tomato mixture over top. This ensures cabbage rolls will be evenly heated and that the flavor is spread throughout.

Bake in 350F oven for 1 ½ to 2 hours. With a fork, test how soft cabbage is after an hour and half. Serve with sour cream!

PAIGE MATTHIE
Charlottetown, Prince Edward Island

The most important kitchen law my Oma taught me was to never waste your food. Never throw away any more than you must and appreciate all that you have, because someday you might know what it actually feels like to be hungry. My Oma grew up in Hungary and Germany during WWII, and at the worst of times her sister was sent out to collect the fat and drippings from the neighbouring apartment blocks so that my great grandmother could make a pot of oat soup for the family.

I know what you're thinking. Oat soup – surely that's just a savoury version of porridge; but I can assure you that it is so much more. It is soothing to the ill, aromatic to the nose, invigorating to the constitution, and tantalizing to the palate. Peasant food has to be all of these things to pass muster, and I think that might be why some of the best and most iconic dishes in the world come from some of the poorest kitchens.

The hardship behind my Oma's oat soup reminds me to appreciate all those who work so tirelessly to produce high quality, organic food on my little island, and inspires me to waste as little as possible and to celebrate the bounty that I've been given. There's a lot of love in this recipe, and I want to thank my Oma, Theresia Julianne McGee (née Wimmi), for teaching it to my mother who taught it to me, and for nourishing our bodies and souls with her endless kitchen wisdom. With some simple recipes in your back pocket, and a knowledge and appreciation of ingredients, you'll never have to go hungry. I think that's one of the greatest gifts that my Oma ever gave to me.

OMA'S OAT SOUP

- 2 Tbsp bacon fat/olive oil/schmaltz
- 2 cups rolled oats (quick oats are also okay)
- 3 Tbsp paprika
- 3 cloves of garlic (or more if you really like your garlic)
- 3 cups chicken/vegetable broth

Simply fry the oats on a medium-low heat in the fat or oil in a big cast iron or high sided pan and add the paprika and garlic after 2 or 3 minutes to release the flavour. Once the garlic aromas have appeared, pour in the stock and bring to a boil, then reduce to a simmer.

In about 10-15 minutes the oats will have softened and absorbed a lot of the spiced broth. It will continue to thicken over time, so add a couple tablespoons of water to each serving as needed and stir while reheating.

NANCY FACCHIN-BELLE
Edmonton, Alberta

This is a story and recipe to honour my Nonna Eugenia.

When we were very young, my dad decided to move our family back to Treviso, Italy where my parents were from. Now my Nonna Eugenia was a do-it-yourself type of woman. My grandfather had passed when my mom was only 13, so Nonna had to raise three girls and make sure there was enough food, clothes and a roof over their heads. While we were staying with her, she cooked from scratch. She also had chickens in the yard. This was all new to us and very interesting; we had never seen this before!

One day stands out to me like it was yesterday: We were in Nonna's front yard, and she said we were going to have fresh chicken dinner tonight. We didn't think nothing of this; we just thought she was going to the store to buy a chicken like we do in Canada. We were wrong!

Our Nonna started chasing the chickens in the yard until she caught one, grabbed the broom she had close by, laid the chicken down on the ground, put the broom across its neck and pulled! Wow! The chicken still had some life in it as it ran around the yard until it dropped. After this, she plucked the feathers off, cleaned it and started to roast it with garlic and white wine in a gas oven until the skin was crispy and the meat was ever so tender.

The recipe is a kicked-up version of what my Nonna made. She is my inspiration behind why I became a Chef, why I love food and this industry.

ROASTED GARLIC CHICKEN WITH WHITE WINE BEURRE BLANC

- 1 whole farm-fresh chicken, cleaned
- 40 garlic cloves
- 1 rosemary sprig
- 1 cup white wine
- salt, pepper, to taste

Put chicken in a roasting pan, with garlic, rosemary, white wine, salt and pepper on the skin. Roast at 350F for about 2 hours, depending on size of chicken. Once fully cooked, take out of oven and let rest for 15 minutes. Meanwhile, prepare the butter sauce.

WHITE WINE BEURRE BLANC

- 3 sticks (1 ½ cups) non-salt butter, cold
- ½ cup dry white wine
- ¼ cup vinegar
- 1 shallot, finely diced
- ½ tsp lemon juice

Cut the cold butter into cubes. Bring wine and vinegar to a boil. Add shallot, and reduce mixture until you have about a teaspoon and a half in the pot. Remove pot from the heat, add one cubed piece of butter to shallot mixture. Stir until melted. Continue to add the remaining butter pieces until well blended. Once all the butter is blended, whisk in lemon juice until blended and serve with the chicken.

SUZANNE BERNIER
Quebec City, Quebec

My mom learned at an earlier age to keep traditional French-Canadian cuisine alive, especially since she was only 16 when her mom passed. Her dad was already gone by then as well. She was a young teenage orphan left with many domestic responsibilities, including making meals.

After she married and when I was born, important customs were already in place, no more so than how we observed Christmas and all the food that was a part of it. This was passed down to me and now my family helps with the preparation as well. One of the main dishes? Tourtière of course!

When it's time to assemble these meat pies, the invitation is sent out! It is typically made around the end of November, then frozen to be eaten at Christmas. Everyone has a part in creating this dish and we have lots of fun doing it. We ensure there's enough for Christmas and some for everyone to take home as well.

Just before midnight mass on December 24th we put the tourtière in the oven and it would bake while we were gone and we'd arrive home to the glorious smell. Add a salad and the meal was complete.

Some people have ketchup with it while others prefer cranberry sauce. We even have had it sliced into small pieces and served as an appetizer before a turkey meal. I find that it's a perfect meal anytime during the year, maybe for you too.

SUZANNE'S TOURTIÈRE

Meat Mixture

- 1 ½ lbs ground pork
- 1 cup finely chopped onion
- ½ cup water
- 1 bay leaf
- 1 tsp salt
- ½ tsp thyme
- ½ tsp ground cloves (to taste)
- ¼ tsp pepper

Preheat oven to 425F. In a sauce pan, brown and drain pork. Combine rest of ingredients and add to meat, bring to boil, and cook until all redness of meat is gone. Cover and simmer for 45 minutes or until very tender. Remove bay leaf. Meanwhile, make pastry.

Perfect Pasty

- 2 cups flour
- ¾ tsp salt
- 1 cup shortening or lard
- ½ cup cold water (or more)
- 1 egg

Mix flour and salt together in a bowl. With a pastry blender cut in shortening or lard. Sprinkle with cold water until dough clings together and cleans easily from the bowl.

Roll out half of pastry on a well-floured surface and line a 9 inch pie plate. Fill with meat mixture and cover with the top crust. Seal and flute the edges and slash top. (Be creative!) Beat an egg into a bowl and paint the top crust with it. Bake in preheated 425F oven for 15 minutes or until golden.

Cool pies and freeze for future use or if eaten right away, turn down oven to 350 degrees and bake for 15 minutes or until heated. Serve with tomato catsup or cranberry sauce. Makes 6 servings

HITOMI SUZUTA
Regina, Saskatchewan

My partner was transferred to Regina, Saskatchewan, from Winnipeg, Manitoba, and I had to look for a job there. I had no idea what a "pulse" was until I did a bit of research prior to my interview with the Pulse Crop Development Board. What I had known as a legume, such as dried beans, chickpeas, fava beans, lentils and peas, were actually pulses.

I got the job and learned about Saskatchewan and the world of pulses. While many would identify wheat as the main crop of Saskatchewan, several years of drought and massive rainfall forced farmers to diversify their crops. Rotating crops with pulses on farmland helps to replenish nitrogen and minerals in the soil. Pulse crops in Saskatchewan began to soar in the late 1990s as the Crop Development Centre out of the University of Saskatchewan produced better seeds for northern climates and business development encouraged exports of crops to countries in Asia suffering from climate change. Saskatchewan is the leading pulse grower by producing 70% of Canada's total pulses, contributing $350 million to the province's export in 2005 (according to AGT Food).

I grew up in a household where my adopted mother made Boiled Pork Hocks and Pinto Beans, Boston Baked Beans, Navy Bean Soup, Refried Beans, Southern Beans and Rice, and Three Bean Salad. When I came to Canada, I learned about the food of multi-cultural Canada, such as Indian Dal, Brazilian Feijoada, Lebanese Falafel, British Mushy Peas, and Hummus. But my Japanese cultural background also has pulses, with some of my favorite being adzuki beans made into anko for mocha, or daifuku and wasabi flavored peas.

MOCHI WITH ANKO OR SWEETENED ADZUKI BEANS

- 1 package adzuki bean paste (purchased in cans or in the frozen section of Asian stores)
- 1 cup mochiko sweet rice flour (glutinous rice flour)
- ¼ cup sugar
- 1 cup water
- ½ cup katakuriko (potato starch or cornstarch for dusting the board)

Freeze the adzuki paste until it is hard enough to cut with a knife into 8 pieces and then roll into balls.

Mix flour, sugar and water together in a microwaveable bowl so it is well mixed. It will be a bit soupy. Cover with plastic wrap and put in a microwave for 3 ½ to 4 minutes. Take plastic wrap off and let cool for about 2 or 3 minutes.

Sprinkle katakuriko on a board. Dump cooked mixture on the board and divide it into 8 pieces. Cover hands with katakuriko to keep the mixture from sticking to your hands and pat each piece into a small pancake. Place a square of adzuki bean paste in the middle of each pancake.

Carefully wrap each pancake around the paste in a ball so it is covered but not oozing out. Cool on sheets of wax paper. Mochi can be frozen once it has been cooled.

JOYCE DOKTER
Bonnyville, Alberta

Wild strawberry perogies were by far the best treat of the summer and my favorite summer memory of growing up. This was a treat that my mom as a child enjoyed in Ukraine too.

Baba Rose, my mom, was the chief cook, and anyone who was not doing anything in particular was summoned to help! It took hours to pick the wild strawberries, but as a kid, you knew how delicious they would taste in the perogies later that evening. After picking, we all pitched in to make the perogies and often competed to see who could make the perfect ones and, I might add, ones that did not leak any juice.

To this day, making these perogies is still one of my favorite things to do; I enjoy making this very rich and delicious dish with my kids and the time we spend together as a family.

Once you taste these perogies you will know they are well worth all the time and effort it takes to make them. More importantly, you will always remember the special times spent with special people.

WILD STRAWBERRY PEROGIES

- 14 cups flour
- 1 heaping tsp baking powder
- 1 heaping tsp salt
- 500 ml + 750 ml sour cream
- 2 cups milk

- ¾ cup oil + ½ cup oil
- 1 ½ cups water
- wild strawberries, cleaned but not washed
- sugar
- cream

Mix flour, baking powder, salt, 500 ml of sour cream, 1 cup milk, ¾ cup oil and 1 ½ water in a large bowl.

After mixing and kneading for about 4 minutes, gradually add 750 ml of sour cream, 1 cup of milk and ½ cup more of oil. Let dough rest.

Roll out small portions of dough and cut with a large round circle cutter. Put a heaping teaspoon of wild strawberries in center of circle. Add a level teaspoon of sugar being very careful not to get it on the outside edges of the dough circle. Fold dough over and pinch to seal edges. Place on cookie sheet lined with a parchment paper or tea towel.

After you have made a dozen perogies place cookie sheet with perogies in deep freeze to freeze. Note: If you leave out the perogies too long before putting in freezer the perogies will begin to leak juice and not seal properly, and when you cook them they will fall apart.

To cook the perogies have a pot of boiling water ready. Add frozen perogies. Boil. When perogies rise to the top of the pot, remove from water and put into cream that has been boiled down.

ANGELINA CONTINI
Guelph, Ontario

My Nonna loved to cook for any occasion, big or small, and if she was invited anywhere she said her thank you with food. The food she crafted with her own hands was her gift to us and we received it with all the pleasure and love she intended it to give. She kept a bit of Italy present in all that she cooked; her culture and heritage always remained in her new land.

Even when she had little to give she found a way to share with neighbours who were struggling on what little they had: she'd make dough, gather garden vegetables and tomatoes and a small piece of cheese. "You can make a nice-a pizza," she'd say, with a smiling heart as she gave.

Nonna always had a large garden and diligently tended to it. It served her well and was a part of her daily life until she fell ill and dementia took hold of her, and now... my heart breaks knowing she can't remember the time she spent there just as she can't remember me. I like to remember her the way she was, in her kitchen and garden, harvesting, cooking, giving and filling her heart by bringing happiness to others with what she could create with her own hands.

She would make Minestra Maritata (wedding "meatball" soup) for every occasion, and fritters made from the flowers of her zucchini plants. Everyone loved them and anticipated a taste when walking through her door.

I believe because of her, I am who I am today. I feel her presence when I bake. I am happiest when I see the joy on the face of the receiver. From her I learned the reward for hard work in giving to others too. I am grateful for my heritage and legacy.

PITEYI OR ZUCCHINI BLOSSOM FRITTERS

- zucchini flowers
- potatoes, mashed
- parmesan cheese
- salt
- milk or water
- flour
- oil

Nonna would prepare the zucchini flowers by lightly brushing off any dirt and then slitting each flower and removing the pistil or stamen inside and giving them a rinse. Once she had cleaned all of the flowers she would tear them into pieces.

Most traditionally use flour in their recipes, but my Nonna used a mashed potato base. She would boil and mash some potatoes and cool slightly, then add to them to create her batter.

Some Parmesan cheese, a tiny bit of salt and some milk or water would be added to the potatoes, then the chopped flowers and just enough flour to form a thick pancake type batter.

Olive oil would be heated in a pan on a high flame, testing it with a small drop of batter. When the oil would bubble when the batter was added she'd begin to spoon out the fritters. The batter was dropped by tablespoons into the hot oil, cooked a few minutes on each side to puff up and turn golden and crisp.

Once browned on both sides, she would lay them into a Pyrex dish lined with paper towels and everyone would enjoy immediately. Too yummy to wait for them to cool!!

ANNA MARINIC
Yellowknife, Northwest Territories

My mom was a great cook; she regularly made our meals from scratch despite limited available ingredients. She managed to make cabbage rolls, baked sausages or crepes in addition to the more regional dishes that included northern fish like lake trout, as well as rabbit and moose. But what I really loved was the caribou meat my dad as a hunter would get. It all began with the hunting and finished back in the kitchen where my mom would prepare it.

Despite feeling like the minority in this predominantly Aboriginal community that I was born into, we were right at home hunting alongside those who did so for many years as part of their tradition.

One time, when I was along with my dad for a hunt, I clearly remember the Hispanic music playing in the vehicle, the ice cracking on the ice road and the high spring sun beating down on us when we came across an aboriginal who was having a challenge skinning what he had hunted. We learned he was a chief hunting on behalf of the elders in his community. What stands out for me was that it was natural to stop and help no matter if it was someone who likely could have shown us much more natural skills. It just so happened that he needed our help this time.

That's what this community was about: helping each other in times of need, and sharing what we had or the skills that we knew. I'd go back again in a heartbeat.

DELICIOUS CARIBOU

- caribou meat
- red wine
- oil

- salt, pepper
- garlic, finely minced

It's been a little while since I've made this particular dish, as I have no access to Caribou anymore; however, I remember freezing the selected piece of fresh caribou meat for approximately an hour, slicing it thinly and marinating in red wine for up to eight hours.

After it was marinated, I would quick pan fry in a little bit of oil. Off heat it was spiced with salt, pepper and quite a bit of finely minced garlic. I often served it with endive lettuce and a starchy vegetable.

MEGAN NEWELL
Pierrefonds, Quebec

Welsh cakes. They are not a cake or a cookie. They are a taste of heritage, family, and comfort!

My maternal grandfather was born in Wales in the UK. He came to Canada after being sent down into the same re-constructed coal mine that had collapsed, killing his father. He chose to come to Canada rather than live and possibly die the way his father had. He loved both his new country and his country of birth until the day he died.

My mother passed on his love of Wales by naming me Megan, a traditional Welsh name that was uncommon when I was born. For as long as I can remember, we would make Welsh cakes on St. David's Day, which is celebrated country-wide in Wales on March 1. Little Megan – that would be me! – would stand on a stool flipping the Welsh cakes, sneaking bits of raw dough. When the batch of Welsh cakes was ready, mum would steep a pot of tea and my sister, my mother and I would enjoy. At the age of two, I scarfed down a dozen!

Now I am a mother of two children, Kailey Bronwyn and Brendan Gareth, whose middle names are as Welsh as Welsh can be. We annually make Welsh cakes to scarf down on March 1.

Coming to Canada may have saved my Grandfather's life and in so doing allowed me to be born a proud Welsh Canadian. Cymru am byth and long live Canada!

WELSH CAKES

- 2 cups all-purpose flour
- 4 Tbsp white sugar
- ½ cup unsalted butter
- 2-3 beaten eggs
- ¼ tsp baking powder
- ½ cup currants, washed and drained
- extra white sugar for sprinkling

Preheat griddle greased with some extra butter.

Blend together flour, sugar and baking powder. Cut in butter until crumbly and stir in currants. Add beaten eggs. Mix well until dough-like consistency.

Roll out dough to ¼ inch thick on a floured surface. Sprinkle with sugar. Cut with a round floured cutter or edge of cup.

Bake on prepared griddle, turning once. Enjoy hot!

LORETO NARDELLI
Edmonton, Alberta

I was born in Edmonton to Italian parents who were born and raised in Italy. They immigrated to Canada in 1958 upon hearing that there was great opportunity there. In my first years of life I grew up in the south end of the city called Bonnie Doon. It wasn't till my first years in school that I truly began a relationship with food.

One of my memories that is so vivid in my mind is making homemade spaghetti with my Nonna and Mom. On Sundays my Nonna would come to visit. Sauce would be stewing on the stove at a low simmer for hours. The aromas of those rich tomatoes, garlic, and basil always woke me up. A favorite thing to do was to get the wooden spoon and scoop up some pulp from the bottom of the sauce pan. Then grab a fresh piece of pagnotta bread, and slather a good amount of that saucy tomato pulp, fold it in half and take a nice big bite. The richness of the tomatoes was fantastic. I could have eaten all of the sauce and bread.

Nonna would arrive and the flour would be flying as eggs, flour, salt and water came together to make a most exquisite pasta, and me turning the crank on the pasta machine to make the spaghetti. This type of spaghetti cooks quite quickly and before we knew it and after much groveling, we were at the table enjoying a wonderful Sunday lunch. These lunches were sometimes accompanied by some heated discussion on religion or what was happening in the world. The spaghetti was so good and the next day even better, fried up in a hot skillet, making it crispy and even more delicious with flavors being intensified by time. This to me is Canada, cultures and food!

HOME MADE SPAGHETTI AL SUGO

Pasta Dough

- 2 cups flour
- 2 eggs

- water, if needed

Put flour in a bowl and make a well in the middle for eggs. Slowly mix eggs and flour, adding water only if you feel the dough too hard. Knead dough until smooth, uniform in color and soft to touch. Cut dough in slices, sprinkle with little flour and pass a few times through pasta machine, turning the knob from 1 to 5, until you have smooth sheets. Let pasta sheets rest and dry a while on a tablecloth, then cut sheets with a pasta cutting attachment.

Sauce

- 2 Tbsp extra virgin olive oil
- 1 can San Marzano tomatoes d.o.p., puréed
- 1 clove garlic, minced

- pinch of chili flakes
- pinch of sea salt
- 1 tsp oregano
- Parmigiano Reggiano

In a large skillet heat oil. Sauté garlic with chili peppers until golden brown, then add puréed tomatoes, oregano and salt. Stir and let simmer on low heat for about 15 minutes, or until desired consistency, stirring once in a while.

To Serve

Cook pasta in salted boiling water for about 8 minutes. Drain. Toss gently with half the sauce in a big bowl. Plate spaghetti. Add more sauce on top and dust with plenty of Parmigiano Reggiano.

LYNDA RAE
Winnipeg, Manitoba

My Viking ancestors immigrated to Canada, settling near a quaint town called Lundar. When my Amma and Afi (grandmother and grandfather) sold the Kristjanson family farm and moved to the city, they brought with them a deep love of Icelandic food and tradition.

You know that you are a true Icelander when your stomach starts grumbling when mom hauls the old Singer sewing machine onto the kitchen table. Why does this prompt a vegetarian like me to reminisce about one of the most unappetizing food traditions from the Land of Fire and Ice?

Memories of a dish called Lifrapylsa, or Slátur, remind me of "home." They help me feel connected to my grandparents and beloved dad, even though they are only here in spirit. Slátur is a mix of finely ground sheep's liver, flour, oatmeal, milk, salt and chunks of suet. Traditionally, this mixture is stuffed into pouches cut from sheep's stomach and hand-sewn together. Thankfully well-worn bed sheets and mom's sewing machine are modern day substitutes.

Once the sewn cloth pouches were stuffed, they were tied with string, pierced with a knitting needle and plunged into boiling water. A few hours later, we would enjoy a traditional feast of Slátur accompanied by potatoes and rutabaga.

Leftover Slátur sliced thinly and fried in butter transform to crisp, golden-brown perfection. My dad enjoyed leftover Slátur for breakfast, fried, and in a bowl of hot porridge with brown sugar and cream.

Although Slátur will not be enough to lure me away from my vegetarian ways, it is an integral part of who I am. I am proud of my heritage and grateful to pass this tradition to my daughters – if not on a dinner plate, then through the magic of storytelling.

AMMA LILJA'S LIFRAPYLSA

- 5 pounds liver
- 2 ½ pounds suet
- 1 quart of milk + 1 cup
- 1 cup water

- 1/4 cup salt
- 4 ½ cups oatmeal
- 4 ½ cups whole wheat flour

Boil 2 ½ to 3 hours. Makes 13 pounds or 8 bags.

JACQUI MASUZUMI
Fort Good Hope, Northwest Territories

I grew up in Radeyilikoe (the Dene name for Fort Good Hope), which means "rapids place/home/house." It is one of five communities in the Sahtu Region.

During the summer it was our family's tradition to stay at the same fishing camp near the Mackenzie River. I recall climbing up rocky hills that shadowed our camp below near the river. When we found spruce boughs on the hill, we threw them down off the cliff. Since our lodging tent had a dirt floor, we placed boughs on it for a more comfortable sleep. We were careful to swim in shallow water instead of the deep parts of the river. We played in the bush, explored various lakes and relaxed on the shoreline. These were truly beautiful worry-free days.

One of the reasons we stayed close to the river was to catch fish. While my pop also went hunting to provide meat for the winter, it was fishing that became the focus most days.

My mom would meticulously prepare the fish before it was either eaten that day or dried to preserve it, since we had no refrigeration. We would eat every part of the fish. Nothing was wasted! The dried fish became one of our staple winter foods.

My pop took clean shaven tamarack boughs to be poles, like a tee-pee, for the fish to be dried on. Old stumps that we picked from along the river were lit to smoke and dry the fish in this lean-to that had spruce boughs around it to keep the smoke inside.

I don't eat dried fish too often, but when I do go back north, it is a food I greatly enjoy.

DRIED FISH

- fish (usually whitefish)
- clean shaven tamarack boughs
- fire!

- spruce boughs
- potatoes (optional)
- onions (optional)

Clean, gut and wash the fish. Carefully cut away the backbone from the belly into one big piece. Slice across the belly (soft part) leaving the skin on.

Assemble tamarack boughs as poles, like a tee-pee, to dry the fish on. Light old tree stumps until smoking.

Place the fish pieces inside the lean-to. Arrange spruce boughs around the lean-to to keep the smoke inside. (The fish is dried carefully attended to over a few weeks until it's bone dry just like in a dehydrator.)

When the dried fish is ready to eat, serve with potatoes and fried onions if you like.

IAN GLADUE

Wabasca-Desmarais, Treaty 8, Bigstone Cree Nation, Alberta

I began eating dried meat as a very small child, but we didn't often eat it because of the lengthy process. Every area had their special meat. Some regions would eat Cariboo. Farther up north, in our area (Wabasca) it was typically moose meat. We made it because it tasted very good, but also it was to provide much needed protein and sustenance through long winter months. Smoking and drying it naturally preserved it for about a year, and killed off bacteria and any mold. Eating it with butter or lard and some salt was the treat!

As long as I remember, it was a delicacy, like gold... but tough to come by. I first learned about it from my grandparents who lived in NWT. I can picture my grandmother, outside, placing thinly sliced meat from hind quarters that contained some fat – typically moose – on branches made into racks housed inside of a tripod/t-pee structure covered in canvas. It was about 7 feet high and 5 feet wide. The process of drying and smoking the meat for two to three days had just begun.

After the meat was smoked and dried, if we didn't eat it already like that, my grandfather, Joe, would often continue with the process to pound the meat on a boulder with a canvas under it, with another rock. Joe was beginning another process of grinding it into what would be pemmican. After around 5 hours it became powder-like. Any of us would happily consume it in minutes this way, or I like adding blueberries to it sometimes too. Traditionally, and the only way, is to always eat it with your hands!

DRIED WILD MEAT

- inside or outside round of your choice of wild meat (you don't want to use fatty cuts as they will go rancid in storage)
- fire!
- meat racks
- diamond willow for smoke flavour

Thinly slice the meat no thicker than 1 cm of each cut. You don't want to have to smoke/dry for extra days!

Build up your fire. You want it hot to begin with, and then wait until the embers and charcoal appear. Allow the smoke to smolder.

Place the meat on traditional triangle-shaped racks. We like to add diamond willow for smoke flavour.

Smoke continuously until the meat loses 75% of its moisture. Occasionally flip the meat to slowly and evenly dry both sides.

Table Talk

- What particular culture do you identify with? Do you have more than one?

- What is one of your favorite cultural/traditional foods? Why is this food so special to you?

- Have you ever been surprised how much you like another ethnic dish? What was this dish, and why was/is it appealing?

- Where and when is the food from your or any culture eaten? What is the significance of the occasion? When was the last time you ate this food?

- Have you ever prepared/cooked a cultural/traditional food? If no, and you want to learn how, who can teach you? If yes, how has the experience made an impact on your food story?

FAMILY

Family doesn't have to include blood relations. Your family unit can be comprised of those people who have stood in the gap when others have not been around or are no longer in your world. Similar in some ways to community, family – no matter who you define as family– is there for you no matter what.

Food is often related to the most important demonstrations of love during family time. This can mean sharing the workload to acquire and prepare the food, togetherness and bonding time, serious and lively conversations, teachable kitchen moments, and finally sharing the food. No matter how complicated or simple the meal, love can be shown in so many ways through a family meal.

ADINA TARRALIK DUFFY
Coral Harbour, Nunavut

As I was growing up, my anaanatsiaq's house was always full of cousins, aunts, uncles, extended family and friends. Like many Inuit, her door was always open, especially to anyone who was hungry or seeking good company and an equally good cup of tea.

Her house often smelled of fresh bannock or some kind of stew, bubbling on the stove. At lunch hour, there was often a crowd of us gathered to feast on whatever dish she served up.

One dish stands out in my memory because of how little I appreciated it at the time: her famous Macaroni and Salmon dish. As a child, I fussed over the crunchy salmon bones that my father absolutely relished and insisted were good for me. "They are full of calcium," he'd say, beaming as he devoured every last bite. I would make faces and fill up on bannock and tea, or sometimes rice pudding if I was lucky.

Years later, after my beloved anaanatsiaq had passed on and I was looking for ways to celebrate my father on his 75th birthday (a man notoriously difficult to buy gifts for), I thought back to the delighted look on his face each time he enjoyed this dish in particular. It could be described as a look of pure happiness; a look of contentment; a moment of delicious reprieve found in spoonfuls of cheesy macaroni, flakes of salmon, and delicate hints of green peas.

I decided I would try my hand at making it. The look on my father's face when I served it to him, his wide smile, his reddened cheeks, his surprised laugh, and both of us near tears, will forever be one of my fondest memories. "Not quite as good as hers," he said, "but close, very close."

MACARONI AND SALMON

- 1 box macaroni and cheese
- 1 can mushroom soup

- 1 tin canned salmon, drained
- 1 can sweet peas, drained

Cook the macaroni according to package directions. Drain water. While still hot, blend the macaroni with the soup, salmon and peas.

Extra cheese can be added if desired, and don't forget to add a whole lot of love!

DORINE KIELLY
Edmonton, Alberta

Isn't it funny how we associate a certain food item or dish with a specific occasion or memory? Subconsciously people have been doing that for years and don't even really realize it. That's definitely the endearing quality of comfort food and how it embraces a special gathering. That's exactly what happened the first time my Mother made the famous Danish Rum Soufflé for our family.

My older brother made such a fuss over this dessert that it soon became his calling card favorite. His adoration for Mom's creative culinary flare was music to my Mother's ears. Well truthfully, we all loved the dish, but for Mom, it was her son's adoration for this decadent dessert that turned a Danish Rum Soufflé into Sonny-Bear's Rum Soufflé.

My bother Ron was the oldest of us four sibs. He was the only boy with a rare joy of living with three sisters. I don't even know how the nickname "Sonny-Bear" came to be, but once Mom called him that it stuck and we've all called him that ever since.

My brother was transferred with his employment a number of years ago and now lives with his family in Texas. Ya'll know where that is... far from good old Edmonton, Alberta. The miles separate us now for most of our special family occasions and gatherings like Christmas, Easter and Thanksgiving, but you always know there's going to be a home coming when Mom pulls out her old tattered and worn recipe book, and it's open on the page of Sonny-Bear's Danish Rum Soufflé.

Welcome Home Bro!

DANISH RUM SOUFFLÉ

- 4 egg yolks
- 3 egg whites
- 1 cup of sugar
- ¼ cup Rum

- 1 envelope of plain gelatin
- ¼ cup cold water
- ½ pint whipping cream
- unsweetened chocolate (Bakers)

Beat egg yolks and ½ cup sugar until lemon colored. Add Rum. Soften gelatin in cold water that's been dissolved in or over hot water. Stir into egg yolk mixture. Beat cream until stiff and moist and fold into beaten egg whites.

Pour into a serving dish and chill 4 to 6 hours or even overnight. Serve garnished with chocolate shavings and maraschino cherries.

This is a great light dessert after a big heavy meal. Enjoy!

VANESSA SAVELLA
Laval, Quebec

Where do I begin to explain what this dish means to me?

During my childhood, my family would often plan outings to the beach and parks for picnics. I remember my mom always making what we Italians call "zucchini frittata" which would regularly become the filling in between slices of fresh bread that my dad would make. This sandwich was my favorite. My mother even used to make it for us to eat when we would travel by car on road trips. It was *always* the food that my father and I would ask for.

Now that I have a family of my own, it's my turn to prepare picnic foods, and the zucchini frittata is back! Not only is it loved by my husband, children and parents, but it brings back memories of my own childhood that I can share with my family.

ZUCCHINI FRITTATA

- 2 zucchini
- 1 onion
- olive oil
- 6 extra large eggs
- ¼ cup of milk
- salt, pepper
- parsley
- fresh basil
- 1 cup Mozzarella cheese
- 3 Tbsp Parmigiano cheese

Chop up the zucchini and onions into small pieces and cook in a non-stick skillet with a drizzle of olive oil until tender and brown. Remove heat and let cool down.

Mix the eggs and milk together and add the seasonings (salt, pepper, parsley and basil). Incorporate the zucchini and onions into the egg batter; add the mozzarella cheese and Parmigiano cheese. Mix everything together.

Cook in a glass pan in the oven for about 40 minutes at 350F.

This recipe is delicious both hot and cold.

JILLIAN DURHAM & JOYCE KLASSEN
Whitehorse, Yukon

When I was younger, we moved to the Yukon, which meant moving into parts unknown, away from our extended family. My dad went ahead of us and eventually found a church that he felt very at home in. When we all walked into that little church, with people from the same traditional Mennonite heritage, it felt very welcoming and familial.

We were soon adopted, through our church, into the traditions of a long-standing family – the Klassens. Our new friends became our Yukon family. We became very close, sharing experiences together in a somewhat isolated community. We quickly started making family memories; we shared holiday meals (when "The Buns" would make an appearance), camping trips, and other gatherings. Joyce and her husband Henry Klassen have been so dear to me that I often refer to them as my "Godparents" because they are so much a part of my growing up.

Years ago at my bridal shower, I requested that each lady bring a favourite family recipe so that I could start my own collection, and this is when I got the Buns Recipe from Joyce. I was so happy! After I received the recipe from her, Joyce taught me and my mom her method of making them. I've been making them ever since; however, as with any good family recipe, it never tastes as good as when the recipe matriarch makes it... but I'm trying.

BUNS RECIPE

- 3/4 cup warm water
- 2 cups warm milk
- 3 eggs
- 1/8 cup sugar

- 3/4 cup shortening (or oil)
- 1 ½ Tbsp active yeast
- ½ Tbsp salt
- 8 ½ to 9 cups flour

Mix water, sugar and yeast, let stand 5-10 minutes. Add milk, eggs, shortening and salt. Mix well. Stir in some of the flour. Add the rest of the flour gradually, kneading it in.

Let rise for 45 minutes, punch down, and then let rise again for 45 minutes. Form into buns. Let rise for 45 minutes more.

Bake 15 minutes at 400F.

NAN TRAINOR
Stratford, Prince Edward Island

It's June 1st – time to get the garden going! The men brake the ground and the women do the rest. We'll have fresh vegetables to look forward to. They'll be enjoyed year round but are most loved in my Boiled Dinner.

Non-Islanders often cringe at the name, but this has been a favourite on the island forever. In the summer and fall we'll savour lettuce, tomatoes, beets, radishes, rhubarb, corn, peas and beans. The rest, I'll freeze. I'll store all the carrots, potatoes, onions, turnip, parsnips, and cabbage (which are the heart of my Boiled Dinner) in the cellar for the winter.

When the weather gets cooler, it's time to make my Boiled Dinner. This tradition has been passed down in my family for generations. Everyone loves it, especially after being out in the cold. I remember how much I liked it because it was good, hot, and full of vegetables and meat. It really hit the spot in the winter after walking over a mile to and from school.

I still make this for my family, especially in the winter. I make a huge pot so we have leftovers. Then I add my own twist: I take out the cabbage, chop the veggies and meat up into smaller pieces, thicken it like a stew, make a biscuit crust for the top and bake it like a beef pot pie. My family loves it this way!

I now make a separate dish for family to take to their homes. I guess they just can't make it like I do. I also make small separate dishes for my friends and neighbours in my senior's complex. I'm not sure why this is such a big deal, but I guess it's because it's made with love.

BOILED DINNER

- beef (or substitute corned beef or cured pork shoulder)
- carrots
- turnip
- parsnips
- onions
- potatoes
- salt and pepper, to taste
- biscuit mix

Cut up the beef (inexpensive steak) or stewing beef and add to a big pot. Cover with water and boil for about half an hour. Coarsely chop the carrots, turnip, parsnips, and onions and add to the pot. Add salt and pepper to taste.

At the end, add the potato – so they won't get all mushy (or cook in a separate pot with broth from the meat and veggies).

The next day, cut the veggies and meat into smaller pieces, and cover with a biscuit mix. Bake in the oven until the crust is cooked and the dish is heated throughout.

TAMRA DAVISON
Vernon, British Columbia

My family and the business that my family is involved in cannot be separated. Davison Orchards is so much part of us... or perhaps you could say, it *is* us.

We've been growing food in Vernon since 1933, when my husband's great-uncle Tom purchased the farm. Farm production first began with apples and then expanded to include other fruits and vegetables.

My husband and I joined the farm full time in 1985. Now, our children are involved. You'll find us in the fields, in the market and in the office. You'll also still see my father-in-law, "Grandpa Bob," motoring around on his quad or telling a story (or five) to farm guests, and my mother-in-law helping out in the bakery or anywhere there is food. Our farm is definitely a family affair and we would have it no other way!

You can be part of our food story with a visit: seeing the crops growing, fruit being picked, and apples being peeled for pie and other delights. We welcome you to come to make your own memories and traditions.

While it is hard to choose just one recipe to share, fall just wouldn't be fall at the Davison home without Apple Baked Squash. I can't remember a thanksgiving gathering without it. Of course, the apples come from our orchard and the squash is picked from our garden. We sincerely hope you enjoy it as much as we do!

APPLE BAKED SQUASH

- ½ of one medium squash (butternut is best), seeds removed, peeled
- 2-3 apples
- ⅓ cup brown sugar
- ⅓ cup margarine, melted
- ½ tsp salt
- ¼ to ½ tsp cinnamon

Cut squash into ½ inch slices and apples into slices and arrange in 8 inch square, glass dish. Combine remaining ingredients until well blended. Pour over squash mixture. Cover with tinfoil and bake at 350F for 45 minutes until soft OR cover with plastic wrap and microwave for 20 minutes. Let stand for 3 minutes before serving.

SHEILA TYSDAL
Saskatoon, Saskatchewan

My story starts on a farm near Briercrest, Saskatchewan, where we farmed for 40 plus years. My family loves their chokecherry syrup. The raw fruit by itself is very sour to the taste and has a large toxic seed inside, but to my family it was like gold. They loved its strong fruit flavor in their mouths as they would dip their morning toast into it, sopping up every last bit on their plate.

First came the picking (which I usually had lots of help for from my kids), then extracting the juice to make the syrup. There were some spots for chokecherry picking close to home, but quite often they were picked over and hard to pick. Then a good friend told me of a road near their place that had chokecherry trees on both sides of the road for many miles. It was wonderful, easy picking.

That was quite a few years ago, and since that time the kids have grown up and moved on and we have moved to an acreage outside of Saskatoon, Saskatchewan. What is so awesome is that our acreage has many rows of chokecherry trees, and our grandchildren are so excited to help pick cherries for nana to make chokecherry syrup.

CHOKECHERRY SYRUP

The first part in making the syrup is to extract the chokecherry juice. To begin with, wash the chokecherries. Place in a kettle and barely cover the chokecherries with water. Boil them for about 30 minutes or until they are soft. Strain the juice (a pillowcase works great) into a container for a few hours or overnight.

Note: Do NOT crush the seeds as they are highly toxic if broken apart!

- **8 cups chokecherry juice**
- **8 cups white sugar**

- **½ package pectin (I use Certo®)**

Boil 10 minutes or to a syrup stage (110F). Pour into sterilized jars and seal with sterilized lids.

Note: Use 1 cup white sugar to 1 cup chokecherry juice.

ROBERT MAILLET
Neguac, New Brunswick

I was raised in a smaller community close to the Miramichi River. It is a very long fresh water river with salmon in it. My dad's side were all fishermen, so when we visited any of them, especially my grandparents, we'd enjoy a fish meal that could include anything from lobster to mussels.

Our immediate family of five expanded tremendously to a very large crowd on holidays or special events, but it was the traditional gathering on Sundays after church that became the highlight of the week, whether it was at our house or at one of our relatives. Grandparents, uncles, aunts and cousins would come for this meal. The cooking was down home and familial. This was a communal Acadian, French-influence cuisine and experience at its core. Potatoes, turnips, cabbage, carrots and other staple vegetables were stewed together with herbs like summer savory. There was also ham or beef as well. If it was lobster season we could easily have three dozen lobsters to feed everyone.

Did I mention that *everybody* would show up?! Lots of talking and sharing about what happened during the week while kids went off playing outside. The food was simple but wholesome, and the conversations very lively.

Now that I have my own family, I recognize this legacy by placing value on the importance of preparing food, and talking and eating together as a demarcation of the day, disconnected from technology and work/life pressures, focused on the time with people that I love.

ACADIAN POUTINE RÂPÉE

- **2 pounds potatoes**
  - ½ washed, peeled, boiled, mashed
  - ½ washed, peeled, grated
- pillowcase (or cheesecloth) to squeeze starch out
- salted meat or rock sugar

Mix mashed and grated potatoes together. Using a pillowcase or cheesecloth, squeeze starch from potatoes. Then roughly make fist-size balls.

In each ball, poke a hole in the center and add some salted meat. Alternatively add a piece of rock sugar for a sweet version.

Seal up the ball. Place balls in boiling water and cook for 20 to 30 minutes. To serve, enjoy with your favorite topping: molasses, brown sugar, sweetened condensed milk, or salt and pepper. You could also just eat it plain!

ASHLEY PHARAZYN
Oak River, Manitoba

When I was growing up, my Nanny and Papa had a hotel in Oak River, Manitoba. Every special occasion we would pack up in Winnipeg and drive the 2 and 3/4 hour journey to where our family would gather. Each Easter, Thanksgiving and Christmas were spent at the Blanchard Hotel. My mum would call before we left, and when we ran through the door ready for hugs my Nanny would have a cheeseburger waiting for us.

During our stay the hotel would constantly be filled with the delicious smell of my Nanny's homemade soups. People would drive in from all over the area to get a bowl of her borscht, cream of mushroom or minestrone. On days that one of those soups was featured people would be disappointed if they missed out on getting a bowl.

When talking to Nanny about those soups I asked her what the secret ingredients were that made people get in their trucks and drive miles to see her. She said that her borscht had a tin of tomato soup, which helped the beets keep their deep colour. Cream of mushroom sometimes had bacon. And minestrone had lots of onions, which were sautéed first for sweeter flavour and better taste.

I am taken back to these visits and family holidays each time I prepare a pot of soup at home. The smell of my simmering bone broth (in the recipe that follows), or onions being sautéed in butter, bring memories flooding back. My Nanny is a fantastic cook. I believe that the outcome, taste and flavours will always be enhanced when the cook is filled with love.

ASHLEY'S BONE BROTH

One of the favorite food workshops I teach is the bone broth class. Everyone is so interested in the broth's healing properties. I also recommend most of my clients have bone broth weekly. Hope you enjoy it too!

- chicken or turkey bones
- white onion, halved
- 2 large carrots
- 2 celery sticks
- ½ lemon
- ginger root chunk
- 2 cloves of garlic
- water

Put all of the ingredients into a cheese cloth and place in a slow cooker. Fill the entire crock pot with water and set it on low. Let simmer for 12 hours. Hint: Start the batch at night to wake up to a house that smells incredible!

TANYA SEVDAGIAN
Montreal, Quebec

It was Valentine's Day 2017 and I was at work. My coworkers were buying chocolates and clients were getting their hair done for their dates. Everyone was in a great mood. One of my coworkers asked me what I was making for dinner. Keep in mind I had a 3 year old, so no hot dinner plans; but at that moment I realized I had *nothing* planned.

I left work early because I wanted to surprise my husband when he got home. In the store I roamed around, then passed the seafood counter. It inspired me to get ingredients to make a seafood pasta, since my husband loves pasta. Due to lack of time, I also bought pre-made Coquille St. Jacques. Since my baby loves strawberries, I bought chocolate-covered strawberries coated with shredded coconut for dessert. Then I rushed to the bus terminal with heavy bags, and as I waited for the bus in the cold, my husband called to tell me he was leaving work soon. I tried to act very casual and told him to take his time!

When I finally got home, I hurried to get things ready and finished just as my family arrived. The people I love the most. My husband, grinning from ear to ear, asked, "What did you make?!" I just told him to quickly change!

We all sat and just enjoyed each other and the food. My husband said it was the best pasta he ever had, including in restaurants. I said it was made from love. We all looked at each other and no words were needed. Then came Apollonia's favorite! Strawberries! Once dinner was done we cuddled on the couch. BEST VALENTINES DAY EVER in my book of memories.

SEAFOOD PASTA

- linguine
- 2 Tbsp olive oil plus more for drizzle at the end
- 3 garlic cloves, minced
- bunch of shallots, chopped
- crab (as much as you like)
- scallops (depending on the size, about 3 to 4 per person)
- 1 large shrimp per person
- chicken broth
- 1 pound of mussels

Boil salted water for pasta. Cook pasta according to box directions.

Fry garlic and shallots together in the oil then add the crab, scallops, and shrimp. Remove them from the pan when cooked.

Add chicken broth to the pan then the mussels. Cover and wait for all the mussels to open. Once the mussels have opened, add the rest of the seafood and cooked pasta.

Toss and plate. Drizzle with more olive oil. Serve.

EDITH YOUNG
Charlottetown, Prince Edward Island

My family grew up eating lobster. My dad was a lobster fisherman as well as my grandfather and many of my uncles.

I suppose you could say that since we ate so much lobster we would gladly eat something different some days. We had an opportunity to do so at school. Many children from lobster families like ours would trade what we had as lunch – that oftentimes would be lobster sandwiches – for whatever else our classmates had for lunch. Yes, we ate that much lobster so we traded it away!

Here is one of the ways we eat lobster. Mix it with cooked pasta, bottled pre-made coleslaw dressing and fresh garden chives. It is a hearty and easy dish to prepare. It is especially very tasty after you let the flavors blend in the refrigerator. Served cold; dinner is ready! Hope you enjoy this dish.

LOBSTER CASSEROLE

- 250 gram package of elbow macaroni
- 1 pound lobster, cooked
- 475 ml coleslaw dressing
- handful of chives, cut up, to taste preference

Cook the elbow macaroni as per packaged directions. Cool. Set aside.

Cut up one pound of lobster. Then combine it with the cooled macaroni in a large bowl. To this bowl, add the entire bottle of coleslaw dressing and mix well. Garnish with cut up chives.

Set in fridge for flavors to blend.

JANET WISZOWATY
Winnipeg, Manitoba

My father's mother was Ukrainian so the meals we shared with my Granny Rudolph were hearty and delicious during our holiday celebrations. My favourites were perogies and cabbage rolls. Then one day I was introduced to some other interesting foods. Some similar but different, and some very new. My husband's family was Polish and ate food that was still in the Slavic arena, but their dishes were from a different array of foods from what I had experienced.

My mother-in-law, like my grandmother, seemed to cook by instinct. She would throw a dish or meal together and it seemed effortless and so delicious. I would ask my mother-in-law for a recipe and she just couldn't give it to me since it was too natural to her. So I would watch her when I got the opportunity. She made the best tomato soup from the tomatoes from her garden. I have not mastered it.

I have many recipes, from my love of soups to my great-great grandmother's shortbread recipe. I have chosen to share one of our family's favorite, Dill Pickle Soup. As I said, my mother-in-law never used a recipe and it was a challenge duplicating any dish. I finally purchased a Polish cookbook. My book of choice was *The Art of Polish Cooking*, by Alina Zeranska. My mother-in-law was visiting one time and noticed my cookbook and the picture of the author on the back cover. As it turns out, she knew the woman! They had been in the same camp after escaping from Poland after World War II. I have adapted several recipes from this cookbook. Here is my adaption of Dill Pickle Soup (Zupa ogorkowa).

DILL PICKLE SOUP

- 6 cups beef broth, homemade or canned
- 2 Tbsp of cornstarch (I prefer it to flour)
- 1 cup of sour cream (I use sour cream instead of milk)
- 4 or more large dill pickles, shredded (I use Polskie Ogorki)
- 2/3 cup liquid from pickle jar
- 2 ½ cups boiled, sliced potatoes

Bring broth to boil. Meanwhile, add the cornstarch, pickle juice and some of the broth to a jar and shake it up before adding to the pot to prevent lumps. Add to the broth, then bring the mixture to a boil to thicken. Remove from heat and add the pickles, potatoes and sour cream and heat. Do not boil.

Serves 12.

HANNA RACZKOWSKA
Toronto, Ontario

When I was pregnant with both my kids, I craved potato-based comfort foods. With my first, living in Montreal, this craving was easily appeased with classic poutine that you could get everywhere, or cheese fries at a fast food eatery. (I know, not the healthiest option for a pregnant woman.) However, with my second pregnancy, these fast foods were nowhere to be found, despite the same craving.

We were living in Northern Ireland, and poutine as we know it in Canada did not exist, and no Taco Bell either. I turned to other comfort foods I made at home, foods my mom had prepared for me growing up, like perogies, potato latkes, and potato dumplings. Our Polish background had a lot of potato options in its traditional meals that I enjoyed growing up.

Since then, we have moved back to Canada (Toronto), but I've continued to make these dishes for my kids. They especially like my potato latkes. There's something special about being able to share a favourite childhood meal my mom used to make for me, and make it for my own two kids. Recently, I made a healthier version, sneaking in some other veggies into the mix, and they were just as good. Happy kids, happy mom.

SPECIAL POTATO LATKES

- 2 large potatoes
- 2 carrots
- ½ of a large zucchini
- 1 onion
- 1 egg
- 1/3 cup flour
- salt and pepper

This dish can be made by chopping onions and grating the remaining ingredients on a fine hand grater. But I prefer to use a food processor, to make a super smooth consistency.

Peel all vegetables. In a food processor, finely chop the onion. Then grate the remaining vegetables in batches and set aside in a bowl. Once the vegetables have been grated, put everything back into the food processor in batches. Using the chopping blade, continue to process until the vegetables resemble a puree. This mixture is then combined with the remaining ingredients in a bowl to make up the batter.

To cook: In a frying pan, add oil and heat it up. Drop tablespoon amounts of batter into the frying pan and cook until lightly browned at the bottom. Flip, and repeat on other side.

Serve with sour cream and top with finely chopped chives.

STACY WESTMAN
Sherwood Park, Alberta

I was eight years old the summer my brother and I moved to the small house across from the golf course. It was only a matter of time until we realized there was money to be had by collecting lost golf balls from the woods that bordered the golf course. It was understood that we could exchange the money for candy at the local drug store.

We would dodge stray golf balls, listening to them crack into the trees, and try to follow their trajectory. It was hard work, for all the tramping through the bushes, over logs, into bogs and out again; but far more exciting to me than the money we earned was the discovery of wild Saskatoon bushes bursting with ripe, juicy berries.

We filled bucket after bucket each summer and took them home, where our mother would wash and pick through them, freeze some for later, and bake some into berry crumbles or make delectable Saskatoon jam. We'd also eat them fresh by the handful, and picking these berries opened up a lifetime love of wild berry picking no matter where we've gone or how old we've gotten.

My oldest son has developed his own love for Saskatoon berries. We have bushes down on the green belt, but he wants to have his own in our yard and I don't blame him. I like making a double-berry crumble in the summers to serve warm with natural vanilla ice cream.

DOUBLE BERRY CRUMBLE

- 2 cups washed Saskatoon berries
- 2 cups washed blueberries
- ¼ cup packed brown sugar
- 1 Tbsp + ¼ cup gluten-free flour, divided
- 1 ½ cups gluten-free oats
- ¼ heaping tsp cinnamon
- ½ cup brown sugar (not packed)
- ½ cup chopped walnuts
- ¼ cup butter, chopped into pieces

Place parchment paper circle on bottom of round 8 inch casserole dish. Mix berries, brown sugar, and 1 Tbsp flour. Pour into dish. Set aside.

Mix ¼ cup flour, oats, cinnamon, brown sugar, and walnuts together in large bowl. Add butter. Work mixture with your hands or pastry blender until butter is worked in evenly. Pour over berry mixture.

Cook at 350F for 30-40 minutes, covering with lid or foil for last 15 minutes. Crumble will be done when berries are bubbling up through the oat mixture and along the edge of the dish.

Serve hot with natural vanilla ice cream. Try it warm for breakfast served with plain Greek yogurt and freshly sliced berries.

Table Talk

- How was love shown during family meals? Was it in sharing the workload to acquire and prepare the food, togetherness and bonding time, serious and lively conversations, teachable kitchen moments, and/or sharing the food?

- What special family gathering involving food stands out in your memory? Why was it special?

- What painful family gathering involving food stands out in your memory? Why was it painful?

- If eating with your family was not a positive experience, how does this impact your food story?

- What is your favorite place to eat together as a family? Is there special meaning attached to this location?

- How often do you gather with family to share a meal?

COMMUNITY

Community is intimately tied to location and the food unique to any given region. Stories of community often involve the food available and grown on the community's land and the distinct ways that the people acquire and prepare it. Conviviality, hospitality, inclusiveness, warmth, support – these concepts all come up many times in relation to food, community, and locality.

Food, community ties, and connections to the land go hand-in-hand. Whether it's by foraging for chick weed in the boreal forest, harvesting mussels and clams on the coast, or farming pulses on the Prairies, we are nourished by nature's abundance as well as the connections with each other and the land.

The sense of home is central to many of the following stories, which capture the way that place is linked to belonging in community. They acknowledge the vital dynamic between food, communion, partnership, harmony, dwelling, and rootedness.

APRIL GLAICAR
Hay River, Northwest Territories

I dedicate this story to the memory of dear Jill Taylor, my fireweed blossom picking beautiful friend.

I am happy to share my favorite wildflower – fireweed (Chamerion angustifolium) – which I've spent the late summers of my life admiring, especially its bright fuchsia flowers, as far back as I can remember. In my travels I've been treated to sightings of this beauty in Alberta, the Yukon and Northwest Territories, including the very tall and also dwarf-like compact (Chamerion latifolium) varieties – depending on the local landscape and climate. My eyes delight at a fresh stand growing in a grassy meadow or a burned out or disturbed patch of soil. One year I even managed to purchase seeds to plant in my yard. Imagine the disbelief of my best friend, a horticulturist, that I would willingly introduce this somewhat invasive flower to my plantings! Yes, we still giggle about that.

A family vacation to Alaska in 2006 yielded a jar of locally made fireweed jelly. Upon testing the light delicate flavour and marveling at the pretty colour, it was decided that I would try to make this treat to celebrate our memories of that beautiful state.

My love of fireweed continues to blossom as I learn about the traditional aboriginal uses of the plants. I'm grateful to have discussed with elders and read reference guides sharing the historical importance of this wildflower. High in both Vitamins A and C, it has long been used in teas, jelly and salad by the people of the boreal regions. Our friends further north and past the Arctic Circle also use fireweed washes for chronic skin issues, and eat the boiled roots for relaxation.

FIREWEED JELLY

- 8 cups fresh fireweed blossoms (no stems) while colour is vibrant – don't wait until they fade
- 5 cups water
- ¼ cup lemon juice
- 1 Tbsp butter
- 2 packages powdered pectin (each approx. 1.75 ounces depending on brand)
- 4 ½ cups white sugar

You will need a cheesecloth for this recipe. Set aside.

Rinse blossoms. Place water and blossoms in large pot (that is large enough to allow for a hard boil) and heat to gentle boil until flower petals turn grey.

Remove from heat and strain through cheesecloth into another pot, only keeping the deep purple juice. If the juice is brown you've used too much water or the flower blossoms are too old.

Heat fireweed juice, lemon juice and butter in this pot to a rolling boil. Add the pectin and return to hard boil – hold for 1 minute. Add the sugar and bring to full boil – hold for 1 minute.

Remove from heat and use a piece of cheesecloth to skim the top of the mixture. Immediately fill sterilized 250ml glass jars to about 1/8 inches from top, place sterilized tops and rings, and tighten. Process in hot water bath for 10 minutes, remove and let cool overnight. Check tops for seal.

COLETTE STASIEWICH
Pincher Creek, Alberta

I grew up in a small, picturesque town nestled in the foothills of southern Alberta. In the far distance there are the majestic Rocky Mountains overlooking our small community. The rolling foothills flatten out somewhat into farmland dotted with cattle, horses, and hay bales. The relentless air swooping off the mountains ranges from gentle breezes to "des vents pour écorner les boeufs," as we would say in French, which means "winds that could rip the horns off a bull"!

In spite of the non-stop wind, I loved growing up in my small town where I felt comfortable and safe with the neighbours who surrounded me. Of course I didn't personally know everyone, but their familiar faces and smiles gave me a sense of well-being and contentment; I could freely walk down any street and feel at home.

It was a carefree lifestyle: long days filled with riding bikes, throwing rocks in the creek and picking wildflowers, my favorite ones being crocuses. I also learned at a very young age that I loved the kitchen, and being from a family of 11 kids, there were plenty of opportunities to develop culinary skills.

I grew up at a time where pretty much everything we ate was homegrown or bought fresh and prepared at home. There were no shortcuts; it was all lovingly made from scratch and it was all delicious. How does a person pick one favorite dish? Simple. Saskatoons.

For as long as I can remember, I loved everything about Saskatoons. The process began as we hurried through the fields, little white buckets swinging, out to the canyon where the low bushes were laden with dark blue, juicy, berries. We spent hours in the sun, picking, eating, and filling our buckets. They were carefully brought home, sorted and washed.

SUMMER BERRY FEAST

- fresh Saskatoon berries
- fresh (farm) cream

- sprinkle of sugar

We began the feast by pouring thick fresh cream over the shiny Saskatoons, sprinkled them with sugar, and then sunk our teeth into them. The big smiles on our blue lips betrayed our groaning tummies. Another perfect day!

BARBARA STEEL
Oro-Medonte, Ontario

This chili recipe came to our table from Sault Ste. Marie some 40 years ago, from a friend whose mother made it regularly. It has become a staple in my kitchen too, and I always have a container or two in the freezer. If a friend or neighbour is in need of a meal for whatever reason, I have some to give to them.

Our community was raising money a few years ago for our local playground and they decided to have a Chili Cook Off as part of the events. I entered my name, cooked up a batch, and of the 13 entries I won "Peoples' Choice Award." Now that's saying something.

Hope you who are reading this book – and try the recipe – will also agree that it is G-R-E-A-T!

CHILI CON CARNE

- 1 lb medium ground beef
- 1 large onion
- 14 oz can diced tomatoes
- 5 oz water
- 1/8 tsp cayenne
- 1 Tbsp chili powder
- 1 tsp salt
- 1/3 cup white vinegar
- 2 Tbsp fat or cooking oil
- 1 large green pepper
- 5 ox can tomato paste
- ½ tsp paprika
- 1 large bay leaf
- 1 clove garlic
- 14 ox can dark kidney beans, rinsed

In a large pot cook meat until pink has disappeared. Drain off fat. Mash into small bits. Heat oil in skillet, sauté onion and green pepper. Add to meat. Add remaining ingredients and stir.

Cover and simmer for approximately 1 hour, stirring occasionally.

JENNIFER ENGLAND
Whitehorse, Yukon

We've lived south of Whitehorse for a number of years now. Our commitment to grow our own vegetables or hunt is fulfilling and nourishing. This commitment is rooted in a deep respect for the boreal forest and how much it offers northern communities. It is also inspired by our local Indigenous friends and communities who have taught us to live more sustainably in short growing seasons.

I've had the privilege of learning from northern food leaders like Boreal Gourmet chef Miche Genest, and popular herbalist and experimentalist Bev Gray. I have adopted/incorporated seasonal and regional treasures into meals, like spruce tips with fresh salmon. As well, activities like preparing fish and collecting and drying rose petal flowers have added to my local food knowledge. Festive shortbread with dried rose petals is a treat for us at Christmas.

I've also become creative with what I first identified as weeds; I spent countless hours trying to weed them out of my garden areas! Edible plants that are naturally found in the boreal forest contain outstanding nutrients. Why battle with the inevitable and prolific patches of chickweed? You *could* feed them to chickens – I'd love to have our own chickens someday – or better yet, eat them yourself!

To keep this superfood on hand, I grind it up and place it in ice cube trays. Once frozen, the chickweed cubes are at the ready to use for something like smoothies.

CHICKWEED SMOOTHIE

- 2 chickweed cubes
- ¼ avocado, peeled
- 1 medjool date
- 1 banana, frozen

- ¼ tsp matcha powder
- 1 1/3 cup almond milk
- handful of spinach
- ¼ tsp vanilla extract

Blend together until smooth.

BERDINA PEDDLE
Job's Cove, Newfoundland and Labrador

I was born into a community that both my mom and dad were raised in as well as their parents. We always had animals like horses, and for food, our cows provided milk and cream for butter. Chickens were raised to give us eggs, and pigs and beef would be processed at the butchers. Since dad was a fisherman we could always count on fish, like salt fish, in the summer as well.

Anyone with big families made bread at least every other day. Ours was no exception with mom baking most days, and if we were running short of bread, we ate a Newfoundlander staple: Toutons!

Often we would rise to the delicious smell of them frying. It wasn't a problem getting up when we were going to enjoy fried bread dough. To add to our morning meal, especially in the winter, we would have hot cereal like rolled oats or maybe an egg with it.

It wasn't just at breakfast that we would eat Toutons. As a supplement to our diet, we'd also eat it with baked beans, pea soup or with anything instead of bread. One of my favorite ways to enjoy it then and now is like a dessert, with molasses!

I have passed this tradition onto my family. While we don't eat it as often as I did when I was young, we occasionally have it as part of a breakfast-type supper with bacon, hash browns and eggs. Toutons are now easier than ever to prepare because you can even buy the dough at stores. They also are available in various restaurants that sometimes serve it with fish cakes or molasses. No matter when I eat it, it reminds me of my upbringing and the area I am proudly from.

TOUTONS

Use white bread dough that has risen overnight.

When ready, break off small pieces the size of an egg and flattened ½ inch thick in the palms of hands. As a traditional method, fry the pieces in fatback until they are browned on both sides.

Serve as a hot breakfast with hot molasses and butter melted in it, or alternatively use golden syrup or marmalade instead.

ADAM MALCOLM
Qikiqtarjuaq, Nunavut

Eating well in the north can be a challenge. All produce is shipped up on little planes. It's very expensive. And by the time it gets here its shelf life is often practically spent. One alternative is to forage for things like berries, tea and edible roots and herbs. I do a little of that in the warmer months. Many from the older generations of Inuit do much more of it.

Another way to put fresh food on the table is by fishing and hunting. But there are obviously limitations to how many of your calories you can get this way. Hunting was a sustainable traditional practice in the north when the population consisted of little nomadic bands of tens of people. Nowadays there are tens of thousands of people in Nunavut, and only so many caribou and whales to go around. On top of that, it is often a long trip by snowmobile or four-wheeler to get away from the community, where game is scarce, to better hunting grounds. The machine, the gun, it all costs money. For many it is simply not affordable. So, perversely, it seems that hunting has become almost a luxury for people here.

The first time I tried northern country food was in the summer of 2011. We were at a camp called Koka on the south side of King William Island. An elder had caught a goose in the morning and brought it back to camp. While gutting, he cut out a kidney and popped it in his mouth. He pulled the second kidney out on the blade of his hunting knife and extended it to me. Not wanting to appear squeamish, I threw it back. It tasted a little like a bloody nose. But good. It was good. The elder smiled and nodded at me, his teeth bloody, and I smiled back. I've eaten a lot of raw organs of a lot of different northern animals since then. I have to say, I've acquired a bit of a taste for it.

JESSE CHAN
Halifax, Nova Scotia

When people learn I'm from Halifax, I often hear comments such as, "Oh, you must love to eat seafood over there such as lobsters, right!?" I always laugh because for me, the real iconic food for "Haligonians" is donairs! Every single time I head back home it's the first thing I get to eat!

Donairs over the past decade have evolved from their original pita form. Now there's donair eggrolls, donair pizza, and even donair poutine. Any time when friends or strangers ask for suggestions on what to try in Halifax, I *always* say donairs. With their incredibly juicy shaved meat, fresh diced tomatoes and onions, warm soft pita bread, and signature sauce, donairs are really the perfect food in my opinion. The sauce is really what makes donairs great! It creates a perfect balance of sweet and savory for this local favourite. Just thinking about it brings up a lot of good memories, such as times downtown after coming from concerts with friends, late nights cramming for exams in university, basketball tournaments, and birthday celebrations.

I'm a proud Haligonian and feel that we are some of the nicest people in Canada. As some would say, "you get to their heart through their stomach." Well, I believe donairs are the perfect food that represents my home city, and that it will win your heart over once you get to try it. My mouth is watering already just thinking about it! You have to go to Halifax and get one!

JINETTE SAVOIE
Inuvik, Northwest Territories

I had the opportunity to live in Inuvik for 1½ years a few years ago, where I worked with children ages 5 to 18 who came from numerous communities out of town. I was like a house mother available for the girls, helping them to settle in and taking care of them. Along with the head lady in charge, we looked after each other in this community within the community.

The larger community was also wonderful and very welcoming. It didn't matter what my background or skin color was, I immediately felt like I belonged. I was accepted no matter what.

As part of activities, we would often go to pick wild cranberries and strawberries that grew on top of sponge-like mossy terrain. It really felt like we were walking on a rug! You'd have to crouch down very low in order to see the berries, since they were hanging almost touching the ground.

It was a beautiful time as well as a cultural immersion. When in town I'd often see caribou hanging up before skinning. I also saw a lot of caribou in the process of being made into jerky (caribou jerky was readily available). Then there were the pots of tea; it seemed like lots of people loved tea! You'd see them sipping it while eating a slice of a bannock-type bread. This bread similar to the traditional type of bannock. Perhaps you might want to make a version of the one I've included with my story.

If I had a chance, I'd go back in a second. I encourage you to visit as well for an outstanding experience.

ESKIMO BREAD

- 2 cups flour
- Pinch salt
- 1 lb shortening
- 2 tsp baking powder
- water

Stir together flour, baking powder, and salt. Add water, stirring until a very soft lumpy batter forms. In a cast iron pan heat the shortening. Drop batter by spoonful into hot shortening and cook both sides.

It can be served for breakfast, or with soup, stew or chowder. It's very delicious, especially when it's piping hot with butter... and with tea of course!

TAMMERA MERKENS
Victoria, British Columbia

I invite you to come on a food journey with me. We live in Victoria currently; however, my food life did not start on the coast of BC, and to my recollection it wasn't until I was ten years old that I was introduced to salmon. I distinctly remember a family meal together when I bravely tried the foreign food. Initially I was totally uninterested, but soon it became a staple and then a household favorite.

Now, as a mother of two young girls, it's so interesting to me how where we live impacts our household food choices, and therefore how we feed our children. When I began to feed them, choosing salmon as a first protein came so natural. Here in BC wild salmon is available everywhere and fresh when in season. It's just a common ingredient on family tables and restaurants.

As an adult the source of our produce and protein has become a passion of mine. Therefore, it is important to me that we purchase wild salmon, as it aligns with our family values.

I love that there are so many different ways to prepare salmon, making it so versatile. Even though I love to have fun with salmon, typically I just go with the simplicity of a little olive oil, salt and a touch of lemon. I feel like this preparation allows the flavor of the fish to sing, particularly when it's fresh!

WILD SALMON

It's important to get the freshest fillets of wild salmon you can buy. This is how we like it prepared.

- **fresh wild salmon fillets**
- **extra virgin olive oil**

- **1 Tbsp lemon juice, fresh**
- **sea salt, to taste**

Line a baking sheet with foil and create a little nest for your fillet.

Tap the moisture off the fillets with a paper towel then coat with the best quality extra virgin olive oil. Squeeze a tiny amount of fresh lemon juice over all the pieces then sprinkle some awesome sea salt over top, to taste.

Bake at around 425F or on the BBQ for about 15-20 minutes.

DEBORAH HUTCHINGS
Cornwall, Prince Edward Island

For the first 18 years of my life, mussels were not part of my food story. Little did I realize then how much they would be a part of my life now! You see, I was familiar with and liked clams, but I never had a bowl of mussels before. This was about to change.

It all began in Venice when my girlfriend and I were wondering what to eat at an authentic Italian restaurant. The attentive grey-haired gentleman who was the owner noticed my glance at the bowl of mussels served to nearby guests. Before we knew it, he came out with a bowl just for us. Somehow he felt my need to try them. With his hands, he gestured that it was to be his treat. And what a treat it was. I remember they were in a tomato base and very delicious!

Years later when in Newfoundland, my husband and my parents had an opportunity to have mussels. In particular, my dad, Wally Patch, who never had mussels but always loved all shellfish, also became a huge fan and continues to be to this day.

Now, living in PEI, I have had mussels seemingly everywhere: at restaurants, friend's houses, and of course in my own home. I'm still trying to duplicate that taste from the first time I ate mussels in Italy; however, we also enjoy them steeped in white wine, butter, or beer. Really, you can't go wrong. How about ginger, garlic and coconut milk? Pear and white wine? Or perhaps shallots, garlic, cherry tomatoes, basil, cilantro or arugula.

The recipe I share is one of the first recipes I used and still use when in a pinch. It reminds me *a little* of that Italian mussel recipe. It can be a company or everyday fare.

MUSSELS SOUP

- butter or olive oil, to cover bottom of pot
- garlic, shallots, or green onions, to taste
- 2 lbs mussels
- 1 cup good quality dry white table wine
- can of tomato soup

In a pot, stir-fry garlic, shallots, or green onions with butter or olive oil. Throw the mussels in the pot and cook them. (The most important thing to remember after the mussels have been cooked is that any which have not opened up are to be tossed, since only the open ones are good to eat.) Stir in wine and tomato soup. Heat through.

Serve it, as the comfort food it is, with crostini or French bread. Put a piece of bread at the bottom of a bowl and ladle the soup over top.

CATHY CLEMENTS
Digby, Nova Scotia

It all comes honestly. Nova Scotia clams and chips.

My dad sold the clams and chips in his canteen in his younger days. My late Uncle Ansel dug clams, and the legacy is carried on by his son today in Digby. They are known as clamers. If you like seafood and visit Nova Scotia, find a restaurant or canteen that serves Digby clams and chips. The clams are dug from the sea bed when the tide goes out and are processed at the local fish plant, where an electrical shock releases the raw clam from the shell. The clams are put into one gallon glass jars and are sold from the fish trucks to restaurants.

If you share a bus ride with a fish plant worker, you know where they work, and the smell lingers on after they get off. With a limited supply there is not enough to export out of the province, and sometimes the restaurants run out of clams.

CATHY'S NOVA SCOTIAN DELICACY

- jar of raw (out of the shell) Digby clams
- Aunt Jemima pancake mix
- salt and pepper

Mix dry Aunt Jemima pancake mix with salt and pepper in a large storage container. Roll the clams in the dry batter until coated.

Deep fry the clams until golden brown. (A dedicated commercial deep fat fryer is used to only fry the clams in, then the oil is regularly filtered to remove the loose dry batter.)

TRACY BARTH
Kamloops, British Columbia

We moved to Kamloops from Spruce Grove, Alberta, in 1994. It was hard leaving family and friends behind. Shortly after moving I won a cookbook contest that, amongst other things, had my recipe included in a Christmas cookbook. The local paper did an article about our family and I was named "Kamloops cook of the week." I did not feel like a stranger in town any longer! It seemed everywhere I went people would say "I know you!"

I started keeping track of my own recipes, adapting as needed to taste preferences, and added family recipes as well. I also sat with my Mom to get her recipes that she never had written down, so that one day my children would have them too. Soon I had a recipe book that was very much my own, which I gifted to each of my children on Mother's Day 2016. Now that they have families of their own they can also start adding the recipes they love, keep that book growing, and one day pass it along to their children.

Living in Kamloops introduced me to salsa. The abundance of tomatoes and peppers makes it so easy to make your own amazing salsa from scratch. Growing up in a home where the summer months were busy canning times, I thought why not develop a recipe that I can preserve for the winter months when there are not as many ingredients to make fresh salsa. I tried several batches and finally came up with this one. It is so much fun getting together every summer in the kitchen – chopping everything by hand – making batches of salsa that everyone likes!

THE BEST SALSA

- 8 cups tomatoes, peeled, squeezed, chopped
- 1 cup or 10 Jalapeno peppers
- 1 cup sweet banana peppers
- 2 cups onions
- 6 cloves minced garlic
- 1 red pepper
- 1 yellow pepper
- ½ cup vinegar
- 1 small tin tomato paste
- 2 Tbsp sugar
- 2 Tbsp salt
- 2 Tbsp paprika
- 1 tsp oregano
- cilantro, to taste
- 2 ghost peppers or 5 habanera peppers, optional

Chop all the ingredients, then add to a large pot. Simmer for 4 hours on the stove.

Put clean sterilized jars in the oven at 250 degrees for 10 minutes. Put the snap lids in boiling water for 1 minute to soften the rubber.

Pour hot salsa into the jars and immediately add the lids and tighten firmly. There is no need to process – the hot liquid and the hot jars will seal the lids down. Ensure the lids have sealed and store in a cool place for up to one year.

No two batches are ever quite the same, given the uniqueness of the hot peppers. Cherry bombs are awesome but not as easy to find. Habaneras work well, but watch the ghost peppers, which are the hottest I have used. Some like the recipe just the way it is without the extra heat, and some like it with lots of kick. Just make sure you use rubber gloves when chopping the hot peppers and jalapenos.

RAEANNE PERRY
Summerside, Prince Edward Island

When I think about food from PEI, there's only one answer: potatoes! Potatoes are as synonymous with PEI as red dirt and Anne of Green Gables. It's what the Island is known for, and therefore there aren't too many islanders that weren't brought up eating potatoes as a regular staple in their diet. There are two ways I could go with this: seafood chowder or chicken fricot (pronounced "FREE-co," and if you can roll your r's like the French, then roll that r!).

While many might be familiar with a seafood chowder, I'm guessing fewer are familiar with a chicken fricot. A fricot is basically a stew/soup, and chicken fricot is a traditional Acadian dish that was served regularly in my home growing up. I always found it funny and odd that the title of the dish is such a mish-mash of English and French; but then if you listen to an Acadian speak these days that's usually what you get, Franglais or Frenglish, so maybe it works after all!

The recipe is easy to make and is good anytime of the year, though it's best in the fall or winter when those root vegetables are fresh and when the cold starts to set in.

CHICKEN FRICOT WITH DUMPLINGS

- whole chicken or chicken pieces
- onions
- celery
- salt
- summer savory (or other herbs and seasonings)
- 4 to 5 potatoes, cubed
- 2 to 3 carrots, cubed

Put the chicken in a large pot. Cover with water. Add onions, celery, salt and summer savoury, and other seasonings you would use for a chicken stock.

Once the chicken is cooked, take it out of the pot, and add the potatoes and carrots. Meanwhile, debone and skin the chicken, cube or shred it, then and add it back to the pot with the vegetables. (You may want to add more salt, summer savory or other seasonings to your taste.) Simmer everything together for a few minutes until the flavours all come together and the root vegetables are cooked.

Traditionally, dumplings are added on top. As a child I hated dumplings so I don't think my mom added them often, but you can!

DUMPLINGS

- 1 cup flour
- 1 Tbsp summer savory
- 2 tsp baking powder
- ½ tsp salt
- ½ cup milk

Whisk dry ingredients together and slowly add milk until a thick batter forms.

Drop a spoonful (1-2 Tbsp) at a time into the soup until they become puffed up. Cover the pot and simmer for another 5 minutes.

CLAIRE SMITH
Yellowknife, Northwest Territories

I grew up in Eastern Canada, Nova Scotia first then New Brunswick on the Bay of Fundy. We always harvested wild foods as kids and I grew up digging clams and picking wild blueberries. My mom used to say I ate three buckets for every one I picked. No food was better than wild blueberries. When I was a teenager we moved to the Okanagan with all its fruit trees, and then to the west coast with its salmon and cultivated berries, but I never found any berries to match my beloved east coast wild blueberries.

In January 2000 my future husband asked me to move north to Yellowknife, in the middle of winter! Adjustments were made, but the beauty and wildness of the North won me over and reminded me of my childhood and the wild foods I enjoyed then. I worked at a small airline that serviced northern communities and people would ask me to send them hard-to-find items. I loved to do this and would often receive amazing things as a thank you, like an entire arctic char frozen whole as it was pulled out of the ice. One day I sent someone seeds for their vegetable garden and they gifted me with a bag of wild arctic cranberries. I was in heaven! Here was a tart, sweet and juicy flavour to rival my beloved blueberries! Imagine a berry with so much flavour and nutrition that black bears and grizzlies will sit and eat them all day!

I am back living on the West Coast, but I still find a way to have arctic cranberries in my freezer every year! Here's my favorite cranberry recipe, exploding with flavour. It can be made when you are camping if you cook it on a baking stone.

ARCTIC CRANBERRY SCONES

- 2 cups all-purpose flour
- 6 Tbsp brown sugar, divided
- 2 tsp baking powder
- 1/4 tsp salt
- 6 Tbsp chilled butter, cut into small pieces
- 2/3 cup + 1 Tbsp cold cream, divided
- ½ cup wild arctic cranberries (frozen work best) or 1 cup of cultivated dried cranberries
- ½ tsp cinnamon for topping

Preheat oven to 425 degrees. Whisk together flour, 5 Tbsp sugar, baking powder, and salt. Cut in butter until mixture resembles coarse crumbs. Stir in 2/3 cup cream until just moistened. Fold in cranberries.

On a lightly floured surface, gently knead dough into a 1-inch-thick large rectangle and cut into equal sized squares. Cut each square into two triangles and place on a baking sheet or baking stone 2 inches apart. Brush tops with remaining cream and sprinkle with remaining sugar and cinnamon.

Bake until golden brown, 12 to 15 minutes. Let cool on a wire rack.

Table Talk

- Where do you call home? How has this place made an impact on what you eat?

- What communities have shaped your food choices?

- How have these communities affected your food consumption?

- Where in the Canadian wilderness are you connected to food? Why is it important or nourishing?

- Where in rural Canada are you connected to food? Why is it important or nourishing?

- Where in urban Canada are you connected to food? Why is it important or nourishing?

- How do you support your local or specific region's food supply, whether wild or cultivated?

COMFORT

Food can comfort and nourish us in many ways. It can remind us of a loved one and the way he or she prepared food for us, like a much needed warm hug. Certain meals can also bring a taste of home, no matter where we now live. Or maybe you found comfort like never before because you moved to a new region and experienced its food; and perhaps this comfort came just as much from the people you were with as from the food itself.

Comfort food often triggers strong emotions, just as strong emotions often trigger the need for comfort food. The stories in this chapter erase any negative connotations of "comfort food," which can arise from a guilt-inducing view of what we eat. No matter whether the comfort food is considered "healthy," it can nourish us by conjuring memories of the past, by honouring the people, the places and the pleasures associated with the food. We don't have to wait until we're sad or in pain to indulge in comfort food; we can keep the joy of memories alive by telling the stories and eating the food that honour the best about our past.

RAY COLLINS
North Sydney, Cape Breton, Nova Scotia

First and foremost, Pat is short for Patricia, and she was my Mom. Mom passed in 1996, but her legacy lives on in her children and grandchildren every day. My mother loved to bake, not just for the family but for everyone. She would start baking every year in the early fall to have all the "care packages" ready to mail before Christmas. Date squares, tweed squares, shortbread cookies and homemade bread– mom would pack the freezer full prior to Christmas and then ship everything out just in time for friends, family and extended family.

She always believed in sharing, especially with those who needed it the most. You see, my mother grew up in an orphanage in Newfoundland in the late 1930s and early 1940s. She knew what it was like to have nothing and vowed that she would do all she could to make sure nobody else felt that way. She could always set another place at the table for someone who needed to eat, or find a bed for someone who needed a place to sleep, no questions asked. I miss my mom every day, but I like to think she instilled some of those values in me and my brothers and sisters.

I can remember coming home in the fall and smelling the applesauce cake cooking in the oven, a signal to us all that Christmas was on the way. It was also a subtle message to look out for those less fortunate and to strive to be better. I am deeply honoured and humbled to share my mom's applesauce cake. Its enticing smell of spices and the richness of its texture will warm your heart all winter long.

PAT'S APPLESAUCE CAKE

- ½ cup butter
- 2 cups brown sugar
- 3 cups flour
- 1 tsp baking powder
- 2 tsp baking soda
- ¼ tsp salt
- 1 tsp each of ground cloves, nutmeg and cinnamon
- 2 cups applesauce (if you can, make your own)
- 2 cups raisins

Cream together butter and sugar. Mix all dry ingredients. Alternate applesauce and dry ingredients into butter and sugar mixture. Fold in raisins.

Pour into greased and floured tube pan. Bake at 300F oven for 90 minutes. Check when it is done by inserting a toothpick into the center. If it comes out clean, it is ready.

This cake is best served after a fall supper with a cup of coffee or tea and some friends. It makes a wonderful gift to a new neighbor or to someone who just needs a friend.

COLLEEN HARLTON
Summerland, British Columbia

Garlic? Not so much a part of my prairie upbringing. Collards or Kale? Never heard of them back then. Root vegetables of all kinds, seasonal fresh corn, freshly shucked peas, sweet garden tomatoes and carrots–now these were what I was familiar with. I realize now how lucky I was that my Mom served our family a variety of vegetables despite the era of meat and potatoes and the impact of processed foods and Kraft food commercials. Our plates were filled with plant-based foods, prepared simply, steamed in water or raw, sometimes with a smattering of butter, salt and pepper. Oh – and we loved our home canned pickles and relishes that filled our pantry, though admittedly, we did enjoy Bick's® pickles now and then. Vegetables, right?

Fast-forward to the mid-1980s, when I moved to Vancouver and fell in love with Portuguese cuisine thanks to my fortuitous encounter with my now husband, whose family immigrated to Canada from Portugal in the 1960s. How did I ever exist without garlic? Baked, chopped, sliced, crushed, or minced. Bring it on! Collards and kale in salads, wraps, smoothies and soups? Yum! Enter my mother-in-law's traditional "Caldo Verde," or Portuguese Green Soup with homemade chourico sausage. Delicious and so versatile, this soup remains a staple and a favorite with our family and friends. A simple swapping and omission of ingredients and it accommodates the palates of vegetarians or vegans. Our comfort food, this soup also makes its appearance at family gatherings and celebrations.

Now, living in the Okanagan for over two decades, we enthusiastically support the local Farmer's Markets, where there is an incredible abundance of the best-ever organic garlic, collards, kale and potatoes. And despite the heat of the summer season, this soup still makes it to our table.

PORTUGUESE GREEN SOUP OR CALDO VERDE

- 6 Tbsp olive oil, divided
- 1 to 1 ½ cups chopped onion
- 2 tsp chopped garlic
- 8 cups water (or chicken or vegetable stock)
- 2 cups potatoes peeled and thinly sliced (Idaho works well)
- 6 oz chorizo sausage thinly sliced
- 1 lb collards or kale, washed, trimmed, thinly sliced
- salt and pepper

In a medium soup pot, add 2 Tbsp olive oil and on medium heat cook onions and garlic for 2-3 minutes until they turn translucent. Don't let them get brown.

Add the water or broth and potatoes. Cover and boil gently over medium heat for 15-20 minutes. Meanwhile, in a skillet, cook sausage until most of the fat is rendered out, drain and set aside. Wash and trim collards or kale, and thinly slice. (Hint: layer and tightly roll leaves together, massage back and forth then thinly slice). Set aside.

When the potatoes are tender, mash them with a potato masher right in the pot. Add sausage to the soup and then add the collards or kale. Simmer for 5 minutes. Add the remaining olive oil (optional) and season with salt and pepper. Ladle into bowls and serve.

MARILYN STRIEMER
Winkler, Manitoba

Many times during and just after the depression, whatever one owned had dual purposes, and recycling was already being done without any fanfare. In that day and age apples came packed in wooden boxes, a precious commodity.

So it was that our playhouse was built with love and little expense, of two-by-fours and apple box boards, with a roof of tar paper and leftover barn shingling. During the summer when school was out, this quaint palace housed dolls and paper doll families. In winter months, it became cold storage for sides of beef, venison haunches and smoked ham hanging from the two-by-four rafters.

Dad would bring in a chunk of frozen venison, and with sharpened knife would shave off curls of meat that thawed in our warm kitchen. Mom, meanwhile, cleaned and chopped the vegetables. As the lard was warming in the cast iron skillet on the wood burning stove, the curls of meat were tossed with flour, salt and pepper in a small paper bag and fried first. Then small amounts of water were added and stirred in occasionally. The vegetables were added after half an hour to the browning meat and the lid put back on.

We savoured the aroma while it was cooking, getting ready to enjoy this hearty and flavourful stew, served steaming from the skillet and eaten with homemade, buttered slices of bread.

WINTER-TIME VENISON STEW

- 1 ½ lb venison
- 2 medium potatoes
- 4 large carrots
- ball of lard (size of a walnut)

- several shakes of salt & pepper
- 1 medium onion
- water, as needed
- flour, as needed

Cut venison and vegetables into pieces. Mix everything together and cook in a large pot until venison and vegetables are tender.

JUANITA WILSON
Boundary Creek, New Brunswick

I was born and raised in Gaspe, Quebec. My mom always made me rice pudding because she knew it was my favorite, so when I would come home from school she would oftentimes have it ready for me to eat. This made me very happy then, and even though my mom is no longer with us, having passed away in 2015, I am happy when I eat it now too.

I would like to share a funny story about the rice pudding in a very sad time: It was March 18, 1984, a day we as a family will never forget. You see, my brother passed away from suicide. This was a very difficult time for us siblings, and for mom and dad. Mom asked what she could make for us and of course I asked for rice pudding.

She made a big pot full so we could all have some, as there were a lot of people there for the funeral. The one funny thing that happened while mom was making the pudding was that she reached into the panty for what she thought was vanilla, but didn't realize until she poured it in that it was cough syrup instead! When we went to eat the pudding she quietly told me that "we all shouldn't have a cough now." I thought this was a strange thing to say, but after we had all eaten our fill she told us the truth. We never let her live it down, and I still laugh about it now when I make my own pudding.

Thanks, Mom, for making this fantastic dish for many years!

RICE PUDDING

- 2 cups cooked rice
- 2 ½ cups milk, divided
- ¼ tsp salt
- 3 eggs, beaten

- 1 cup raisins
- ½ to 1 cup brown sugar
- 1 tsp vanilla
- 1 Tbsp butter

Combine rice, 2 cups milk, and salt in pot over medium heat; cook and stir until thick and creamy. Stir remaining ½ cup milk, raisins, beaten eggs and brown sugar into the rice. Stir constantly. Cook for a few minutes until eggs are set. Remove from heat.

Stir in vanilla and butter into the pudding. Enjoy!

ALANA HEBERT
Edmonton, Alberta

This story is about my Grandmother, Alice Sproxton. She has been the motivator and the biggest reason that I have adopted a love for cooking and a joy for feeding people. Unfortunately, Alice has been battling Alzheimer's and dementia for the last five years or so. While her mind is elsewhere, her legacy of recipes have been acquired by many members of her family; but even more so, these recipes have come into my life and have re-invigorated my love of being in the kitchen.

My Gramma was an accomplished baker and never had any expectations of perfection from any of the kids while learning the basics. She was eager to show each of us how to cook, make jam or even wash berries. She always had stories of when she was a little girl, about helping her mother or sisters in the kitchen. We were all astonished when she told us that most of her cooking was done on a wood stove or without any running water. That seems almost impossible in this day and age!

The recipe from her collection that I have chosen is simple, basic, but delicious. This recipe has been my go-to for all occasions where and when I need to bake goodies or show up to feed some hungry bellies. I still have the original recipe that my Gramma Alice handwrote, and it hangs on the side of my fridge, anxiously waiting for me to make another batch.

CHOCOLATE CHIP COOKIES

- ¾ cup white sugar
- ¾ cup brown sugar
- 1 cup unsalted butter (not margarine), softened
- 2 large eggs, beaten
- 1 tsp vanilla

- 2 ¼ cup all-purpose flour
- 1 tsp baking soda
- ¾ tsp salt
- 2 cups chocolate chips
- ½ cup to 1 cup chopped pecans or walnuts (optional)

Pre-heat oven to 375F. Mix sugars, butter, vanilla and eggs in a large bowl. Stir in flour, baking soda, and salt. The dough will be very stiff.

Stir in chocolate chips and nuts, if you're using them. Drop by rounded tablespoon (I use a small ice cream scoop), two inches apart onto a greased cookie sheet.

Bake 8-10 minutes or until light brown. They may appear underdone but if you leave them in too long, they will be tough and crispy. The centers will be soft. Cool completely, and then remove from cookie sheet.

MARGARET BOSE JOHNSON
Langley, British Columbia

Oma and Opa's place was magical. Their small family farm near Langley, BC was a kids' paradise with meadows and climbing-trees, haylofts, goats, and geese.

Every year we looked forward to "Chicken Butchering Day," as exciting as any festival. The day started with Opa coming from the barn, each hand gripping a couple squawking chickens by the feet. He laid a feathered body over the big old stump. Oma raised the axe – one smooth 'Whack!' and off flew the chicken's head.

For us children the fun had started. Headless chickens flopped and flailed in a gruesome but comic death dance, and it was our job to catch them. Peals of laughter and a party atmosphere prevailed as we ran after those flapping chicken bodies, trying to grab them by the feet. They were heavy – we needed a firm grip on their smooth warm legs to carry their awkward weight to Oma, tending the cauldron of water at the campfire.

We watched in fascination as she dipped each headless bird slowly into the scalding water, the pungent odor of boiling feathers wafting through the air. Oma's strong hands then stripped the feathers in huge wet handfuls from their slippery skin. Our job was to remove any remaining pinfeathers. After the first squeamishness we tackled our task with gusto, nimble fingers plucking out every ornery little stub.

The adults gutted and cleaned the chickens, and we scrambled off to play. Our reward at suppertime was always a huge pot of homemade chicken soup made from the necks, feet and egg stocks. Chewing on the gelatinous feet and fishing for the tiny boiled yolks are culinary pleasures that were far more appealing to me then than they are today, but I still love a big bowl of comforting chicken soup.

MOM'S CHICKEN STOCK

- 1 large chicken carcass
- 4 quarts water
- 2 to 3 stalks celery, cut into chunks
- 2 to 3 large carrots, cut into chunks
- 1 large onion, quartered
- 2 bay leaves
- 2 to 4 whole star anise pods (or 3 to 4 whole cloves)
- 1 tsp whole black peppercorns
- 1 Tbsp salt (optional)

Put all ingredients into a large stockpot or slow cooker. Bring to a boil, then reduce heat, cover, and simmer for at least 2 hours and up to 24, or cook in the slow cooker for 8 to 10 hours on low. Strain, then cool. Pick through bones and remove any bits of meat to later add to soup. Discard bones and vegetables. Extra stock freezes well.

MOM'S CHICKEN SOUP

- 8 cups chicken stock
- 4 cups diced vegetables (1 cup onion + 1½ cups carrots + 1½ cups celery, or 4 cups combined vegetables of choice)
- 2 cups (when cooked) starch (2 cups raw diced potato, ½ cup raw rice, or 1¼ cups small uncooked noodles)
- 1 to 2 cups diced, cooked chicken meat
- 2 to 4 Tbsp chopped fresh parsley (optional)

Bring stock to a boil, then add diced vegetables and potatoes or rice. If using noodles, add them 10 minutes before the soup is done. Return to a boil, then lower heat, cover, and boil gently for 20 to 30 minutes until vegetables are tender and starch is cooked. A few minutes before soup is done, add parsley if using. Taste, and add more salt and pepper if necessary.

Makes 8 to 12 servings.

ALEXANDRA AGNESSI
Vaudreuil, Quebec

I have had a love for food from a young age. I was always watching the food network and wanting to explore the ingredients shown that were not always available in my home while growing up.

I come from a background of Greek/Cypriot heritage and have always been influenced by the flavors of the Mediterranean. Olive oil, fresh and dried oregano, mint and lemon would perfume the home on most days. These flavours bring comfort and memories of my childhood that I now pass on to my children. Now with that come endless ideas and recipes with just the base of lemon alone. What's not to love about lemon? It's fresh and can infuse its flavor into anything. This brings me to my choice of recipe to share.

It's a traditional egg and lemon soup, a Greek version of the beloved chicken soup. I remember being very sick at home as a child, not being able to go to school, and my mother would make a batch of this bowl of comfort. Its smell alone will make you feel so much better about the day. My children and husband say it's their favorite soup now; and it's not only used when one is sick, but just for those soup kind of days.

When I eat this soup I feel connected to my mom, whom I lost at a young age; but her memory lives on in our home through food, when talking about her, and seeing pictures of us together.

GREEK CHICKEN SOUP

- 3 lb whole chicken or chicken pieces
- ½ cup uncooked white rice (we use Arborio)
- salt and freshly ground black pepper, to taste
- 3 eggs, beaten
- 2 lemons, juiced
- 1-2 celery stalks, cut up (optional)
- 1-2 carrots, cut up (optional)
- 1-2 potatoes, cut up (optional)

Place chicken in a pot, large enough to add water and other ingredients to it without spilling over. Cover and bring to a boil. When boiling, reduce heat to low and simmer for 45 minutes to 1 hour, skimming the fat from the top as it collects.

When the chicken is done, the meat should pull from the bones easily. Transfer the chicken to a large bowl and set aside to cool. Add the rice, and all other veggies from the ingredients above that you choose to use and season the broth with salt and pepper. Simmer over low heat for 20 more minutes, or until rice is tender. (Any variety of potato works as long as you add them 20 minutes before soup is cooked to not have them turn to mush.)

Whisk the eggs with the lemon juice in a bowl. When the rice is done, turn off the heat. Whisk one ladle full of hot broth into the eggs slowly so the eggs do not curdle. Gradually whisk in more broth until the egg mixture is heated. Then pour the egg mixture back into the pot, whisking fast. The result should be a creamy, cloudy looking soup. You may season with additional salt, pepper or lemon juice at this point. Also all the cut up chicken can be added now.

Enjoy and indulge with a loaf or crusty bread of your choice.

NATALIE GINGRAS
Lac La Biche, Alberta

One of my fondest food memories comes from my grandma. She was Italian and there was nothing better than her homemade spaghetti sauce. (We were really lucky if she also made gnocchi.)

I will always remember going to the farm to find pasta hanging on racks all over my grandparents' tiny farm house. There was never really a recipe for gnocchi, as grandma just knew how to make it using four main ingredients: potatoes, flour, egg, and salt. I remember watching her as we made gnocchi together and how happy spending that time with her made me. It still makes me so happy.

She would keep older garden potatoes specifically just for gnocchi. She would boil the potatoes, and after they were cooled she would put them through a ricer. I still think they look like worms! She would add an egg to the potatoes and then the magic happened. Slowly adding flour to the potato mixture – there were never any measurements – she just knew by feel when it was ready to roll out and cut. I always asked her, "How do you know how much to add?" and she would tell me with her smile and laugh, "My Natty, I've been making this my whole life so I just know!" My job was to roll and cut the gnocchi.

Now that I am older and my grandma is no longer here to make gnocchi, my mom and I make it together and talk about how good grandma's was. Even though our sauce and gnocchi don't taste quite like hers, the memories are always there. I can hear her laugh and feel her love with us... guiding us.

GRANDMA'S SPAGHETTI SAUCE

- 1 onion, chopped
- ¼ cup oil
- ¼ cup butter
- celery
- garlic
- 15 oz can tomato paste
- 2 cans water
- 1/8 tsp cayenne pepper
- 1/8 tsp dried basil
- 1/8 tsp dried marjoram
- 1/8 tsp oregano
- salt and pepper, to taste
- chicken legs and thighs (optional)

Fry the onion in oil and butter, then add celery and garlic. Combine all of the ingredients in a covered roaster. Cook at 350F in the oven for 3-4 hours, stirring occasionally. This spaghetti sauce is wonderful served over gnocchi!

GHISLAIN SAVOIE
Tracadie, New Brunswick

During my childhood our family was constantly moving around eastern Canada. However, no matter where we lived, we always took one trip every year to visit my dad's family in New-Brunswick.

We traveled for 16 hours on the road from Oshawa to Tracadie, hardly stopping on the long drive there. No matter what time we would arrive, even at 2 am, my grandmother Ruby would have a feast for us to eat of everything you could imagine... always nourishing. Even today, in her 80s, she always offers company a buffet! My grandmother is always up for the workload of making all sorts of pies, plenty of canned goods like chow chow, mustard beans or lobster paste, and something from the catch of the day we bring her. We are well fed at granny's!

Amongst the leftovers in my grandma's fridge you could probably find some Fricot (stew). In her younger days, during the long winters when the fishermen weren't fishing much and the loggers weren't logging so much, some families had to depend on the autumn harvest kept in the cold potato cellars or mason jars. Since these root veggies could be grown, preserved and deliciously cooked into such a wholesome meal, you could probably find a Fricot brewing on quite a few stoves. It's one of those homey-feeling meals that takes you back to a simpler time.

Recently with friends, we talked about our traditions and history. I found out that my grandma's Fricot was a bit more interesting than I had thought. I enjoy eating sushi or quinoa salad, but there's just nothing like the taste of home. It's amazing how far a home cooked meal can take you!

ACADIAN CHICKEN FRICOT

I thank my good friend Nikki Vienneau, who combined recipes from both her grandmothers into this one. We share similar backgrounds.

- 10 cups chicken broth
- 1 or 2 cups water to thin the broth (if needed)
- 10 chicken drumsticks
- 1 yellow onion, chopped
- ½ regular cabbage, cut into big cubes
- 1 Tbsp ground savory
- salt and pepper, to taste
- 1 cup turnip, cut into big cubes
- 3 carrots, sliced
- 2 cups white potatoes, cut in big cubes
- 1 cup flour
- 1 tsp baking powder
- pinch salt
- ½ to 1 cup cold water

In a large saucepan bring broth, water, drumsticks, onion, cabbage and seasonings to a boil. Reduce heat to medium. Cook uncovered for 40 minutes. Add turnips, cook 10 minutes more. Stir. Add carrots, cook another 10 minutes. Then add potatoes and cook another 5 minutes.

In a mixing bowl, mix flour, baking powder and salt. Gradually mix in cold water with your hands or a fork to form a ball of dough. With a spoon make small balls of dough of approximately one inch in diameter. Slowly drop balls of dough on the surface of the stew. Make sure to leave 1 to 2 inches apart for expansion. Cook another 10-15 minutes covered over low heat.

Fricot can be prepared with or without the dough. If you choose not to include the dough, the stew must be left to cook for 20 minutes after adding the potatoes, not just 5. Leftovers can be frozen! Enjoy!

Serves 6.

DEBBIE SMITH
Newmarket, Ontario

My mom and grandmothers were wonderful cooks. There was always home baking and home preserves in the cupboard and freezer. When my kids were little, in my younger days, I tried to keep the cupboard and freezer filled too. These days very little spare time, less entertaining, and calorie counting sometimes deter me from this lifestyle, but I have always loved a good butter tart!

I have lost both my grandmothers in years gone by, and just recently my mom in 2017. One thing I will really miss is my mom's baking when I would visit her. I am glad I have received a full box of her recipe book collections. When looking through this box for an appropriate choice for my food story, I saw this square recipe. I think it is the next best thing to a good butter tart! It is a favourite at reunion picnics that our family tries to attend to every year.

My mom and her sister, and my sister and I, held butter tarts very dear when we were growing up, and the love of them continues to this day.

BUTTER TART SQUARES

- ½ cup butter, cut into pieces
- 1 cup flour
- 2 Tbsp white sugar
- 2 eggs
- 1 ½ cups firmly packed brown sugar
- 1 tsp vanilla
- 2 Tbsp flour
- 1 cup raisins
- ½ tsp baking powder
- ¼ cup chopped walnuts (optional)

Preheat oven to 350F.

Cream butter in a medium bowl until smooth. Combine flour with white sugar. Then blend with butter until incorporated and mixture is smooth. Transfer to a 9-inch square pan, spreading evenly. Bake until lightly brown, about 15 min. Set aside. Retain oven temp at 350F.

Combine eggs, brown sugar, remaining 2 Tbsp flour, vanilla, and baking powder in a large bowl. Mix thoroughly. Stir in raisins and walnuts. Spread evenly over crust. Bake until golden, about 25 min. Let cool completely before cutting.

CHERYL HART
Kelowna, British Columbia

Many years ago, our family was blessed with Kelsey, a beautiful baby girl. Her birth mother knew that, despite how painful it would be to let her go, adoption was in the baby's best interest. I am the adoptive mom. Soon after Kelsey came home from the hospital with us, I had my first opportunity to meet her birth grandparents, Andy and Judy, who also suffered the pain of letting Kelsey go. Our hearts immediately connected with theirs, and ever since then they have been family.

Grandma Judy is a much better cook than I, and my most memorable lesson from her was how to make fresh cherry pie! My family is privileged to live in Kelowna, BC – the Okanagan – land of fruit trees, vineyards and lakes. Judy and Andy live in Ohio, and one summer they travelled west for a vacation. Our family enjoyed an afternoon of picking fresh cherries in an orchard. Nothing is sweeter than a juicy, freshly picked, sweet Okanagan cherry!

The next day was pie-baking day. After the messy job of pitting cherries, my youngest daughter, Amy, and I made pie crusts while Judy taught Kelsey how to make the filling. The aroma of cooking cherries filled the kitchen! That delicious filling was poured into each of the waiting pie crusts. Instead of a regular lid cover, Judy worked her magic and created a perfect lattice top for the pies. Later that evening when the pies were cooked and cooled, we dug in to enjoy the most delicious cherry pie I had ever tasted!

As I write this story, Grandma Judy is battling cancer. We are praying for a happy ending and hoping that this summer will bring another opportunity to make cherry pies together.

CHERRY PIE

- 4 cups cherries, pitted with juice (light coloured cooking cherries are best, but any will work)
- 3 Tbsp corn starch
- 1 cup sugar (might need a bit more, depending on the cherries)
- ¼ tsp almond flavour
- uncooked pie crusts

Combine all ingredients except pie crusts in large pot on stove over medium heat. Stir often. Heat until mixture boils and thickens.

Pour into uncooked pie crusts. Bake at 375F for 50 minutes.

Recipe makes enough for one deep dish pie. Double batch makes enough for regular sized pies.

ROSIE HEATH BOCK
Fogo Island, Newfoundland and Labrador

When I was growing up, most of our meals came from what fish my dad caught. My hard-working father was a fisherman in this remote community, an island part of the larger group of islands of Newfoundland and Labrador. It was where I was born and lived for the first 14 years of my life. Ours was a large family (I have lots of brothers and sisters) with strong ties and Christian values. We didn't have much in the way of material goods, but we felt supported and loved with most of our relatives living in close proximity.

Things needed to be shipped to this island, which could get costly. It was difficult to grow vegetables on the mostly rocky terrain; however, because of dampness, we found wild fruit like bakeapples as well as many other berries.

Our menu often consisted of different kinds of seafood, including fish, salmon, and lobster. We also ate a traditional Brewis meal made from hard bread, cod and potatoes, with fried pork and onions served on top. The fishermen would often take these ingredients on their long deep-sea fishing trips. It stored well and became the base for their meals, and ours on land as well.

When I was older, I moved to Alberta to attend college, and have stayed ever since. I have tried to pass on the tradition of this meal to my family, adapting it to suit ingredient availability and tastes. If I can't physically get back to Newfoundland I can be taken back with my memories in an instant when eating this meal. It is a special part of my heritage and a taste of home.

FISH, BREWIS AND SCRUNCHIONS

- hard bread (hardtack biscuits)
- salt fish, like cod
- pork (salted pork rinds or fatback), fried
- onions
- potatoes
- seasonings like salt, pepper, and savoury

Place hard bread in a pot, and cover with water. Soak overnight until softened, around 8 hours. In a separate container, cover the fish with water and soak overnight to remove excess salt content.

The next day, drain the fish and boil it in fresh water until tender. In a separate container, boil the bread until tender. Both fish and bread should be done in about 30 minutes.

While fish and bread are cooking, peel potatoes and boil until softened. When fish, bread, and potatoes are finished cooking, drain all, and debone the fish. Set everything aside but keep warm.

Fry the pork rinds and fatback until crispy. Remove from pan and leave the drippings. To the same pan, add onions and fry until completely cooked. Add the fish and bread to this mixture as well along with any seasonings.

To serve, add potatoes to plates along with fish, bread and scrunchions mixture. Enjoy hot!

NAFISSAH RAMAN
Montreal, Quebec

When the sky is gray and it rumbles, what do we think as a bangali? Kichuri! When your child is sick, what do you make for them? Kichuri! When you are student and it's your first time cooking, you make Kichuri. It's a comfort dish.

The stories are many behind this dish. When you are hungry and don't know how to cook, you call your mom and she tells you to just cook daal (lentils), chaal (rice), and make kichuri. There you go. Your life is saved by kichuri and your homesickness is gone!

For some of us, kichuri is a tradition. You eat it every Friday because you put together leftovers from the past week and make it into a kichuri. When Ramadan comes, to keep your stomach from going nuts, you eat "jaow" (soft kichuri). This dish is versatile and there isn't a right or wrong way to make it. Some like it liquid while others like it firm. At the base, kichuri is a dish made of rice, spices and lentils. The kichuri could be cooked in so many ways: you could add different types of lentils such as mung dall, chaana dall, etc. You could add vegetables or different types of meat.

The word kichuri is even used in daily life to describe difficult situations. When a bangali says my life is a kichuri, it means it's very complicated. Or if someone says it's all kichuri, to me, it means I don't understand anything.

KICHURI

- 1 cup rice
- ½ cup red lentils
- 1 tsp cumin powder
- ¾ tsp coriander powder
- ¼ tsp chili pepper, to taste
- ½ tsp turmeric powder
- 2 bay leaves (Indian kind)
- 1 medium onion, thinly slice
- 3-4 garlic cloves, thinly slice
- 3-4 Tbsp vegetable oil
- 2 cups water

Wash all the dry ingredients together. Once washed put oil, spices, onion, garlic salt and bay leaves together. Mix well and then add water.

Cook on high heat until boiling and the water has reduced to almost half (where you could see the rice). Reduce heat to medium heat and cover until the end. You might need to add more water, little by little.

Serves 4.

SHANNON COURTNEY
Kensington, Prince Edward Island

Our home was perched on a large hill overlooking a patchwork valley of greens and gold near the north side of PEI. The forests that surrounded us were the best playground a child could ever hope for. My dad designed and built the house himself, making the most of what nature provided. He still lives there, almost four decades later.

As a child, most of my daylight hours were spent outside, since mom didn't let us watch TV. As it turns out, mother knew best, and most of my enduring childhood memories are of our outdoor adventures, including picking wild strawberries.

I can't say when my older sister, Sara, and I first discovered the huge wild strawberry patch that would become our daily destination each sunny day in early July for several years, but I remember its location precisely. It was a ten-minute walk through the woods behind our house. After what seemed like ages, we'd emerge into a large, grassy expanse that we called "the back field." This was where we found a patch of wild strawberries growing near the tree line.

We'd squat down and put our silver bowls on the ground, then start diligently picking the tiny red gems. Our sweet dog, Dudley, would oversee our efforts, occasionally interrupting for a pet behind the ears. When we tired of the task, or the mosquitoes got to be too much, or all the ripe and tart sun-kissed berries were gone, we'd trek back to the house with our treasures.

To this day strawberries hold a very special place in my heart, partly because they're just plain delicious, but mostly because when I eat them, I'm taken back in time to those strawberry summers on our little mountain paradise in the woods.

WILD STRAWBERRY TREAT

- **wild strawberries**
- **milk**

- **sugar**

Mix all together in a bowl and enjoy!

Table Talk

- What food gives you comfort? Why is the food comforting?

- What emotions do you feel when eating comfort food? How often do you eat food that is comforting?

- What particular occasions call on having comfort food available? Why is it important to eat this food at these events?

- At what time of year is it important for you to eat comfort food? What is the significance of this time of the year?

- Is it important for you to be in a group of people when you eat comfort food or do you prefer eating alone? Why or why not?

- Who has provided you with comfort food? What impact has this person (or persons) made on your food story?

LIFE

Life. The day-to-day challenges, triumphs, and hilarious events. The transitions and rites of passage. The transformations, whether planned and welcomed or unplanned and painful. As we explore our food story we often discover that food was important at every stage of our journey, marking our daily path as well as the major milestones.

As you dig into your food story, your memories may swing like a pendulum from a low food experience to a high and then back again. On the other hand, it could also be that you do not recognize any particular challenge or incredible pleasure related to food. Your food story might seem fairly bland and unexciting.

Whatever the case may be, your food memories and overall food story offer insights into what nourishes you (or not) along your journey, as you experience the uncomfortable, happy, mundane, even embarrassing moments of life. Discover what is nourishing to you, and acknowledge what is painful, so that you can live like never before.

NARISSA SINGH
St. John, New Brunswick

University life. Can anybody relate to being away from home and *trying* to feed yourself while on a very limited budget? It was a little tough to say the least. There was certainly not a lot of going out to restaurants. Most of the time we ate at home or at the cafeteria if necessary.

I grew up in a family where our mom cooked excellent meals. It was not my responsibility to prepare even the simplest foods. Since my mom did it all, I didn't know how to cook for myself when I landed in a new country miles away from where I was born in the Caribbean.

Both my brother and I attended the University of New Brunswick. For a time we lived together and the burden of cooking was shared between the two of us. Our favorite? You guessed it, the infamous Kraft® Dinner! What truly saved us in some ways were the International Student's Association potluck nights that we were a part of. This was when my brother and I decided to bring Caribbean-influenced food to share. It was somewhat of a challenge to find the salted fish ingredients we grew up with, but even more challenging was trying to get the accompanying bread dough texture just right.

The bread turned out rock hard. Tempted, my brother threw it against a kitchen cabinet, not even putting a dent in the bread. That's how hard it turned out! However, our friends loved what we brought. It disappeared so fast! (I suppose they didn't know any difference anyway.)

Today, I have learned how to cook (very well, my family and friends tell me), but my brother and I still chuckle about that bread!

SALTED FISH DISH

- salted fish packet
- olive oil
- yellow onions
- tomatoes, seeds removed
- fresh thyme

- flour
- baking powder
- salt
- butter
- water

Boil the salted fish to get the salt out. Then flake it. Sauté the fish together with the oil, onions, tomatoes and thyme. Set aside.

Knead together the flour, baking powder, salt, butter and water, and form into balls. Roll out into a circle and fry until golden brown on the outside. Bread should puff up while frying, which leaves it a bit hollow inside.

Slice the bread open – like a pita pocket – and add salted fish mixture inside the pocket. Serve.

MEHGIN REYNOLDS
Kyle, Saskatchewan

My family and I farm in southwest Saskatchewan, and to me farming is about so much more than the crops we grow or the livestock we raise. It's about providing food for my family. One of the main ways I do this is by growing a massive garden and by preserving its produce for winter or later indulgence.

We start our herbs in the greenhouse and then move them into the garden once they are established. Basil in the garden grows like a weed. Last summer I had a 30 foot row full of five different varieties of basil, enough to fill a bathtub. How do I know? Well let me share a funny story.

As a farmer I check the weather about three to five times a day. One afternoon I realized we had a frost warning on for that evening. I didn't want my basil to go to waste so I harvested it all and brought it inside to store while I worked on removing the leaves for use in making pesto. The only place I could store the basil was in the bathtub of our tiny farm house. I was about an hour into stripping basil plants when my husband got home. He walked through the door and asked what that horrible smell was. I was taken rather aback by his comment when he started sneezing. His sneezes were followed by watering eyes and a trip to the medicine cabinet for his inhaler. Apparently he is allergic to flowering basil and I filled the whole house with it. Oops!

PESTO

- 8 cups fresh basil, packed down
- 2 cups pine nuts, toasted
- 16 cloves garlic
- smoked sea salt, to taste
- pepper, to taste
- grated Parmesan cheese (1/2 cup per 8 oz. jar)
- 2 cups olive oil, to preference

Mix all the ingredients together except the olive oil. Then add it to get it to the consistency that you want!

I am a huge fan of garlic. If you do not share my enthusiasm then feel free to cut back on the amount in the pesto recipe. Also, toasting the pine nuts adds a subtle smoky hint to the flavour mix.

If you're planning on freezing the pesto, only add the Parmesan cheese after thawing; otherwise add it to the mixture to eat fresh.

Pesto has a low acidity so traditional canning methods should be foregone. Instead, keep your pesto preserved in the freezer! If you take a jar out to use and don't use the whole jar just top with a quarter inch of olive oil and store in the fridge.

REBA WEBER
Toronto, Ontario

My friend and I shared an apartment for a short time in our early 20s. You could say that we were Hamburger Helper® fanatics! Mainly, the beef stroganoff package mix. We loved it, and usually made it a couple of times per week. It was quick, easy and cheap! We thought that it was healthy because we had to cook it on the stovetop, unlike pizza or something frozen to pop in the microwave. What else are you going to make when you're single and broke? We could get it at the dollar store, so we bought lots of it every pay day.

Strangely, since then, we've both been diagnosed with celiac disease. My diet these days is about eating real foods with none of the food coming from out of a package or box.

One day I was missing that yummy beef stroganoff taste so I came up with this free-from-gluten recipe. This recipe (which is modified from a few others I've found online) is so easy to make and really doesn't take any more time than the box variety does. I just love it. It certainly hits the spot!

BEEF STROGANOFF

- 2 Tbsp coconut oil or extra-virgin olive oil
- ¼ cup onion, diced
- 2 cloves garlic, diced
- 1 ½ lb beef tenderloin or sirloin, cut into thin strips, or ground beef if you're on a budget
- 1 cup cremini or white button mushrooms, sliced
- ½ cup full fat coconut milk
- 1 zucchini, spiralized

Sauté the onion and garlic in oil until the onion is translucent.

Add the beef and brown it through.

Add the mushrooms. Once the mushrooms are starting to soften, add the coconut milk and simmer at a low boil for about 10 to 15 minutes, allowing some of the liquid to boil off.

Add the zucchini and stir it in. Try not to overcook the zucchini. But no matter what, it will still be yummy!

LEEANNA BINDER
Summerland, British Columbia

My fascination with nutrition really began many years ago when our daughter took sick. As a baby, she had eczema all over her body, dark circles under her eyes, and asthma. She truly looked like she was in death's grip. Her body almost immediately strengthened when she was taken off dairy; it was amazing to see her constitution improve so dramatically as a result.

Since then my interest in nutrition and whole foods – in particular plant-based foods – has become even greater. I've lost count at 200 the number of nutrition books I have acquired. You know, when your mom passes away at a young 59 from cancer (as well as other family members), you want to do everything possible to support and care for the body.

It's amazing how something as simple, delicious, and fresh like cherry juice can help to prop up the immune system; or for some, how removing nightshades – peppers, eggplant, potatoes and tomatoes – can calm inflammation and give their body a chance to recover. This is what I've learned and have witnessed many times, both in my personal life and now professionally with clients in my business.

One of the easiest ways I ensure that my body is receiving stellar nutrition is by drinking fresh, pure, unadulterated juice from plants like vegetables, fruits, and selected herbs. Juicing is an easy daily routine that our whole family enjoys. The benefit is tasty juice with heaps of nutrients! If you've never tried juicing before, I encourage you to try this recipe as a "beginner's juice." It's one of our favorites. Enjoy the immediate effects of absorbing premium nutrients which support killer cells that fight off culprits that can attack your immune system.

GREEN JEWELL JUICE

- 4 to 5 leaves kale
- 2 handfuls spinach
- whole cucumber
- 5 celery sticks
- 1 green apple
- ½ lemon
- 1 little piece fresh ginger
- 4 to 5 sprigs parsley

Try to find seasonal and local ingredients. Have everything washed and ready in a big-size salad bowl. Juice. Enjoy immediately!

CORY & MANDY WOYTKIW
Devon, Alberta

For us, vegan has to be quick and simple. We decided that our recipes had to meet three criteria:

1. The ingredients had to be found at our local grocer, in our small town in Alberta.
2. The recipe had to be simple and quick.
3. The recipe had to result in a dish that is epically delicious for everyone to enjoy!

This recipe for vegan Alfredo made with bucatini pasta – Mandy's favorite pasta shape – hits all three successfully, and allows us to eat healthy and satisfy our cravings for comfort food that pop up from our pre-vegan days.

Cue Cashew Alfredo sauce.

It is terrifyingly simple, and every single omnivore we have presented it to has lapped the bowl empty. It takes 20 minutes to make and has no dairy substitutes or nooch (you know… scary vegan stuff)!

BUCATINI ALFREDO

- 1 cup raw cashews
- 3 garlic cloves, freshly crushed
- 1 small shallot, rough chopped
- 1 tsp black peppercorns
- 1 good pinch grated nutmeg
- 1 tsp apple cider vinegar or lemon juice
- 1 tsp sea salt
- 2 tsp potato starch
- 3 ½ cups nondairy milk, divided
- brandy or Canadian whisky (optional)
- pasta
- flax oil

Place cashews, garlic, shallot, black peppercorns, nutmeg, apple cider vinegar or lemon juice, sea salt and potato starch in your favorite high speed blender. Cover with soy or almond milk (about ½ cup) and blend until totally smooth.

Add blended cashew mixture to a medium sized pot with remaining nondairy milk and stir over medium heat until smooth. We like to add a shot of whisky or brandy while cooking for an extra bit of flavor

We pat our favorite pasta with flax oil when saucing (instead of butter). Serve with broccoli, mushrooms, spinach. Top with a little shot of your favorite oil if you like it a little rich and buttery. Consider adding crushed chilies and fresh tomatoes too. Use gluten free pasta for a great gluten free dish.

Make it for someone you love today. It's good for them.

ANGELA O'NEILL
Winnipeg, Manitoba

I have always been passionate about living life to the fullest since I was a little girl. I believe that all my experiences have shaped my purpose. One experience, in particular, led me down the path to where I am today: helping others to eat well-balanced and nutrient-strong meals. Now I recognize it as the best thing that ever happened to me.

I was blessed with the opportunity to learn about holistic health at a young age. I remember writing papers in school about topics of interest, and I chose health. It was around that time that my dad married a lovely lady who had a practice in natural medicine. I was introduced to a healthier way of living that became the norm in our house. At first it was difficult getting used to this massive change – it made me feel very uncomfortable at first – but eventually, I began to adapt to it.

When I was older, in high school, I decided to eliminate sugars and anything processed, which meant I usually brought my own food and water along when I was with friends. As part of this diet, I needed to drink a lot more water than I was used to. I was glad when I discovered infused water blends, which helped add flavour to my water while cleansing my body at the same time.

One of my favorite blends is a recipe I created. It helped me to drink more water then, and I still consider it a great refreshing drink option. Maybe you will too.

INFUSED WATER

- water
- fresh lemons and limes
- pinch Himalayan salt
- fresh ginger, peeled

- cucumber
- fresh or frozen berries
- mint leaves

Add all the ingredients in a large water jug. Adjust the amounts to your preference. You can fill a water bottle with this infused water and take it with you on the go, or drink it fresh at home!

MICHELLE WRIGHT
Smoky Lake, Alberta

I can't recall the first time I made brownies, but I do know that every time I've made them they just aren't the same as the way my Mum did. Not as chewy, chocolatey or satisfying as hers. Could be my pans were too shiny, or maybe the recipe wasn't exactly the way she did it, but something was always off. And because I'm not as satisfied by any brownie the way I am with hers, I'm constantly trying samples everywhere, like my own Holy Grail quest for an amazing brownie taste.

The recipe is so simple; it must be the cook's special something that takes it to amazing. It's a good analogy to life: different people, with what seems to be the same ingredients in the recipe of life, create such different journeys. Sometimes it's the lesson I've learned along the way that's provided the flavor. Just like the time I tried to melt the butter and cocoa and eggs together in the microwave as a short cut. Some life choices don't always give us the results we want!

What I bring to my life, my perspectives, my curiosity, my hormones or my sweat, alters the ingredients I might have, to make my own uniquely satisfying adventure. And where the ingredients do differ, the difference in the journey can be astonishing. So while I am on the quest for that unique taste that was Mum's brownie, I know that my pursuit of my best life is so much more than what I've been given as ingredients. It is my essence that is the unique influence on the recipe.

BROWNIES

- 1½ cup flour
- 2 cups sugar
- 1 cup salted butter, melted

- 2 large eggs
- 2/3 cup cocoa powder
- 1 tsp vanilla, optional

Preheat the oven to 350°F. Grease a 9-by-9-inch baking pan.

In a medium bowl, combine the flour and sugar. Set aside.

Melt cocoa and butter in small sauce pan. Allow to cool. In a bowl, whisk together cooled cocoa and butter with the eggs. Add this mixture into the flour mixture, stirring until just combined.

Bake the brownies for 25 to 35 minutes, or until a toothpick inserted in the center comes out clean.

LOIS DUDGEON
Darlingford, Manitoba

We were raised on a farm near the rural village of Darlingford, Manitoba, just north of the US border. There were eight of us in our family, including our parents. We all had chores with different responsibilities assigned to us, like baking.

I can still smell the cake baking. After all, I made *that* cake countless times. It was one of my jobs, to bake some cake for our school lunches. As the oldest of five girls, we each had our pick of treat to bake that would be included in our lunch. One sister chose chocolate chip cookies and another created jelly rolls. I chose cake, and my go-to cake of choice was Jiffy White Cake with Coconut Frosting.

Our one room school house had at best 20 students in grades 1 to 8. You'd think this was 100 to 150 years ago, but tiny hamlets and areas like ours still existed in the 1960s. We needed to go to school somewhere until we were bussed into the larger town of Morden when our school finally closed.

It was quite the experience to get used to attending a very large school. I clearly remember that this was when I no longer took a lunch pail or box to school. I was not going to be seen with *that* country-girl-lunch-carrying tote in hand. No, thank you, a paper bag would do. I was not going to be embarrassed! However, the treats remained in our lunches, along with the obligatory sandwich and a piece of fruit. I believe that's when I first began to like coconut, and I am still quite fond of coconut today too.

Hope you enjoy!

WHITE JIFFY CAKE

- 1 ¾ cups flour
- 2 ½ tsp baking powder
- ¼ tsp salt
- 1 cup sugar

- 2/3 cup milk
- 1/3 cup shortening, softened
- 1 egg
- 1 tsp vanilla

Mix and sift dry ingredients. Add wet ingredients. Beat with egg beater until smooth. Bake at 350F for 30-35 minutes.

COCONUT FROSTING

- 6 Tbsp melted butter
- 4 Tbsp cream

- ½ cup brown sugar
- 1 cup shredded cocoanut

Blend together well all frosting ingredients except shredded coconut, then stir in the coconut. Put frosting mixture on cake while still warm. Place in oven until it bubbles and browns slightly under broiler, and in a jiffy it's ready for school lunches the next morning.

KATIE ROBERTSON
Toronto, Ontario

When I was growing up, we lived below the poverty line for most of my childhood. My mother was a single parent of two children and suffered greatly from mental illness and addictions, making it difficult for us to eat a balanced, nutritious diet at the best of times. She always did what she could, though that included trips to the food bank as often as they'd allow and visits to the local "greasy spoon" as a treat once in a while. But the one memory that stands out in my mind the most is, on good months, my mother would make a spaghetti sauce.

This sauce was chock-full of meat and vegetables, and it was always a day-long process to prepare; it became a very special way for us to bond and, if even for a day, we pretended like we didn't have to worry about when we'd eat the next nutritious meal.

This is the recipe as I remember it and how I make it, as a special treat for my friends and family, still today. All of the measurements are generally guidelines. I usually just add pinches of this and dashes of that, and when other veggies are on sale (like zucchini) I'll add those too.

MOM'S SPAGHETTI

- 1 lb ground beef
- 1 green pepper
- 1 red pepper
- 2-3 medium-size carrots, peeled
- 1 package white mushrooms
- 1 medium-size onion
- 2-3 cloves garlic
- 1 can tomato paste
- 1 can chopped tomatoes
- 1-2 cans tomato sauce
- 1-2 tsp each thyme, rosemary, sage, and basil
- 1 bay leaf
- salt and pepper, to taste

Pan-fry ground beef until 2/3 cooked, drain and return to pan, add spices and cook fully. In a large sauce pot, on low-med heat, place all the tomato ingredients, and then add the meat. Finely chop all the vegetables (use a food processor if you want to hide the goodies from picky folk) and add to the sauce.

Bring to a simmer, cover and lower heat, simmer 4-6 hours, stirring occasionally. Serve on any kind of pasta and sprinkle with parmesan cheese. Freeze remainder (can freeze up to 2-3 months).

NATASHA TREMBLAY
Montreal, Quebec

This Chicken Detox Soup is one of my daughter's favourites, which is fantastic because I have found myself knee deep in the picky eater phase. Finding sneaky ways to fill her up with vegetables can be a challenge, but the beauty of this recipe is that all the veggies are in plain colourful view and she gobbles it up anyway, excitedly calling out the veggies she picks up with her spoon.

Not only am I a mother, I am also a wife, and the kitchen is my favourite room in the house. I take pride in my food, even if every attempt in my kitchen is not successful, and I put a strong emphasis on presenting my family a meal that also looks beautiful so that they recognize I made them a meal with love. I believe that the goal of cooking really is that the people you are cooking for thoroughly enjoy what they are eating. Who better to cook for than those you love the most?

CHICKEN DETOX SOUP

- 2 Tbsp olive oil
- 1 onion, chopped
- 2 large carrots, chopped
- 3 celery, chopped
- 2 zucchini, chopped
- 1 cup mushrooms, chopped
- 5 cloves garlic, chopped
- 10 cups low sodium chicken stock
- 2 tsp turmeric
- 2 cups chicken, cooked and shredded
- 1 can chickpeas drained and rinsed
- 2 bay leaves
- 2 cups spinach and or kale
- ½ cup ground oatmeal
- salt/pepper, to taste

Sauté onions, carrots, celery and zucchini about three minutes. Add mushrooms and garlic and sauté again for about three minutes. Add stock and turmeric followed by shredded chicken, chick peas and bay leaves. Adjust taste with salt and pepper. Finally add in kale or spinach and bring to a boil, then down to a simmer for about 1-2 hours.

At the end, once all the veggies have softened, ground ½ cup oatmeal in a blender or food processor and add slowly to the soup to thicken it up.

CHERYEL GOODALE
Edmonton, Alberta

Retired from my career and with more time on my side, I wanted to enhance my more than fifty years of cooking and baking for my family by trying new recipes. I was motivated by Loretta's Sprout Natural online posts not only to try new recipes but to concentrate on the importance of planning, prepping, and preparing nutritious snacks and meals. She encouraged me to add in foods that were new to me and start shopping for fresh foods locally.

On a visit to my extended family in Saskatchewan, I learned about lentils – a new food to me – that my niece and her husband grow on their farm. I also learned that Saskatchewan farmers produce about 95 percent of Canada's lentils, and that I was missing out on the nutritional value of lentils in my diet.

I adjusted one of my favorite recipes, a soup we typically eat in the winter, by adding lentils to it. Winter Lentil Soup, a dish that I can prepare at my convenience, simmers in the slow cooker while I go about my day. It is a wholesome meal for family members coming and going, and perfect to have ready for out-of-town guests without an exact time of arrival.

It is refreshing to learn more about healthy eating in our retirement years. My lentil soup is but a small step to nutrition as we continue to learn and change.

WINTER LENTIL SOUP

- vegetable stock
- carrots
- turnips
- parsnips
- zucchini
- celery
- onions

- small potatoes
- tomatoes
- lentils
- kidney beans
- hot pepper flakes
- sprig of rosemary or thyme

Add vegetable stock to a slow cooker.

Chop carrots, turnips, parsnips, zucchini, celery, onions, small potatoes, and tomatoes. (We like to use fresh vegetables from local markets for the best taste.)

Add the vegetables and the remaining ingredients to the slow cooker. Stir to combine.

Simmer on low – 7 to 10 hours – until ready to serve.

TERALEE CHORNOHUS

Langley, British Columbia

I am always amazed at how food can take us back to a place that wraps us up in the warm comfort of memories. Most often those memories are of our childhood. Sometime those memories are of our children's childhood. Either way, food plays a large role in our "feel good" memories.

When our boys were little, they loved to help in the kitchen. There was usually more flour on the floor than the bowl, and it would leave me wondering if it was worth it. But the giggles they made as they ate their creations was always worth the mess. I would try to find recipes that were easy for their little hands to help with. A certain cake soon became a favourite not only because it tasted good, but because it was so easy. There are no eggs to crack. No sifting required. Every ingredient can be unceremoniously dumped into a bowl and stirred to their hearts content. The only thing better than eating it was watching it being made.

Our boys are now grown, but often for family meals I find myself making their favorite cake. It is so easy to make, yet has such a moist, rich flavor that you would think it was much harder to make. Sometimes I serve it warm with ice cream. Other times I sprinkle chocolate chips on top so they bake into the top. Another time I might just let it cool, then dust it with some icing sugar. If the occasion is special, I make a caramel icing that complements the chocolate with a melt-in-your-mouth precision.

To me, this cake reflects the best in life. That the most decadent things can also be the most simple. What makes food truly special is the people that we get to share it with.

WACKY CAKE

- 1 ½ cups flour
- 1 tsp baking soda
- ½ tsp salt
- 3 Tbsp cocoa
- 1 cup sugar
- 1 Tbsp white vinegar
- 1 tsp vanilla
- 5 Tbsp oil
- 1 cup cold water

Mix together all the ingredients and pour into an ungreased 8x8 pan. Bake for 35 minutes at 350F.

NO FAIL CARAMEL ICING

- ¼ cup butter
- ½ cup brown sugar
- 2 Tbsp milk
- ¾ cup icing sugar

Melt butter and sugar together. Cook for 2 minutes, then add milk and stir till boils. Remove from stove, and let cool. When cool, add icing sugar and stir till well mixed. Spread over cooled cake.

SARAH FORRESTER WENDT
Charlottetown, Prince Edward Island

I am one of the oldest of ten children, born and raised on Prince Edward Island. A number of decades ago my dad was diagnosed with Non-Hodgkin lymphoma. At the time we didn't know how much this would be a turning point, not only for my dad and his diet, but our family as well.

The turning point came when my ill father and two older brothers went to Florida, where he attended lectures on macrobiotics for two weeks. As a result, upon returning home he immediately changed his diet to incorporate certain foods, and so did we all. This decision improved his health dramatically, and at the same time made an impact on me.

As a result, it became my preferred way of eating that led me down a career path to practice culinary arts and experience different food around the world; I became a sous chef and eventually a head chef; and I spent two semesters in Mexico and another in Italy. I have also returned a few times to Massachusetts to continue my in-depth study about the macrobiotic lifestyle.

Today, I am grateful to be the head chef of my own whole-foods based restaurant, where everything is fresh, local, and organic. This way of eating has also triggered an interest in food and nutrition in my own children, which for me is very fulfilling.

One of the foods we love is lentils. My mom uses them in a nourishing soup, one of my favorite ways to enjoy this legume. I consider it my go-to comfort food any time of the year.

LENTIL SOUP

- 1 cup dried green lentils, sorted and rinsed
- ½ cup barley
- 8 cups water
- 2 small onions, diced
- 2 cloves garlic, minced
- 2 carrots, sliced in rounds
- 2 small potatoes, peeled, chopped into small cubes
- 2 stalks celery, chopped into small pieces
- ½ cup tomato puree
- 1 Tbsp curry powder
- 1 tsp sea salt
- 2 Tbsp soy sauce
- ½ cup fresh parsley, finely chopped

Soak lentils and barley for about 1 hour before cooking.

In a large pot bring water, lentils, barley, onions and garlic to a boil. Turn down heat and let simmer for 45 minutes. Add vegetables, tomato puree and spices to pot and simmer for another 15 minutes. Stir every few minutes.

Serve hot, topped with parsley and accompanied by homemade bread or pita.

BETH GORBET
Thorhill, Ontario

One of the legendary stories in our family centers on chicken soup – a staple in the freezer, even if only for medicinal reasons.

It was a special occasion and my mother was having a "crowd for dinner." (That is exactly how she spoke.) Since she was a master chicken soup maker, this seemed like an ideal start to the meal. She had this, she was a pro, having served it many times before. Besides, she had a reputation to uphold, so she wanted to serve one of her specialties.

She nursed that soup: using the very best of ingredients; taking special care to skim the top from time to time of the cloudy material that tends to accumulate in order to refine the flavour; using chicken bones and just the right kind of onion and fresh herbs to add depth and richness.

The final task in the preparation was to strain the vegetables and bones from the broth. She would first pull out all the large chicken pieces to save for a chicken salad later, and then the bigger bones. Once separate from the broth, she planned to pull the best vegetables to serve in the soup itself.

Confident in her every move, my mother prepared for the straining by placing a fine colander in the sink, lest she spill a drop. As she proceeded to pour, she heard a gurgling that was not a normal part of the process. The soup went directly… down the drain. That's right, she neglected to place a pot under the strainer and voila, no soup for dinner!

I make my mother's soup often – almost as well as she does – and you can bet that I always remember this story at a most critical point in the preparation. It makes me remember her loving care every time.

T'S CHICKEN SOUP

- 4 lbs chicken pieces (I use carcasses and breasts)
- 14 cups water
- 2 medium cooking onions, scored with an "x" on the top
- 1 Tbsp salt (I use less)
- 3 carrots, cut into pieces (I use more)
- 3 celery stalks, cut into pieces
- 2 parsnip, cut into pieces
- handful fresh dill, minced
- handful fresh parsley, minced

Rinse the chicken and the bones. Combine these with the water and onion in a large pot. (A special soup pot with a strainer is ideal for this. I keep the bones separate from the edible parts of the soup.) Bring the water to a boil and lower the heat to medium for 1.5 hours. Skim from time to time, removing the accumulated cloud that rises to the top.

Add the vegetables and herbs, cover and lower the heat for 1 hour.

Remove from the heat. Separate the chicken and vegetables from the soup and strain (with a bowl or pot underneath!).

Once cooled, the fat can be removed; however, a little fat adds to the flavour tremendously. Add the vegetables back to the soup and enjoy. Cut in chicken if desired; add rice, noodles, or whatever you have on hand.

Table Talk

- Have you ever changed an eating habit or your diet because of someone else's transformation? If so, why was it so powerful?

- How did your home life while growing up dictate what food was available to eat? What stands out as significant?

- Who do you invite to share a meal or drink with you when you want to acknowledge a life moment (whether high or low)? Why do you choose them?

- What specific food(s) have you included to bolster your diet? Who was instrumental in introducing you to this food? How does this food choice affect your daily routine (with family or roommates, if applicable)?

- When did you learn from a mistake while preparing food? How has this experience made an impact on your food story?

CELEBRATION

You can spot a celebration in almost every story in this book, but in this chapter we shine a light on those celebratory times. Stories of watermelon heads, donair parties, secret sauces, special bowls, bonfires on the beach – all of these tales highlight how central food is at the most joyful times of life. They are invitations to share in the celebration!

Nourishment doesn't have to be boring. There's nothing bland about feasting, happiness, and excitement! Celebration doesn't have to be a noisy and busy affair, though. There is cause for celebration in seemingly ordinary events, like picking seasonal garden produce.

When we tell our food stories we realize that celebration goes hand-in-hand with thanksgiving, and that it can be a regular part of our lives. We don't have to wait for a special occasion or holiday event. We can celebrate anytime, whenever we recognize the pleasure and plentifulness of food and are willing to express gratitude, whether loudly in a party or quietly in a garden.

PAM ROBERTSON
Halifax, Nova Scotia

I've lived in several areas of Canada, and there is a food highlight to each of them. I love to see how competitive some regions are when it comes to their favorites, like those delicious donairs in Halifax. My friend Bev's home became my go to family spot when I lived in the Maritimes. Often, Bev's Mom would bring a giant tray of bacon-wrapped Digby scallops, or her Dad made platters of giant log cabin potatoes. We ate, laughed, and ate some more.

One of the hallmark occasions at Bev's was her annual donair party. Her cozy bungalow would be filled with people, letting themselves in the front door and entering the mingling smells of oregano, garlic, and onions. Bev's husband Brady would be in the kitchen slicing the meat perfectly thin and then browning it lightly as people lined up to get the tasty treats. It wasn't just the taste of amazing homemade donairs that brought people, of course; it was hanging out with people you like, and the chance to swap a few tall tales over a plate of great food.

When you create a donair, you can cook your meat in a bread tin like you would a meatloaf, or shape it into a loaf and cook it on a broiler pan (that funny blue thing that came with your stove), or place it on a foil-lined cookie sheet. Just make sure that however you decide to do it, you squeeze everything together as tight as you can so it can be sliced thin without crumbling once it has cooked and cooled.

DONAIR MEAT LOAF / DONAIRS

- 2 pounds lean hamburger
- 1/2 cup breadcrumbs
- 1 tsp ground pepper
- 1/2 to 1 tsp cayenne pepper, to taste
- 1/2 tsp oregano
- 2 tsp paprika (I like smoked)
- 1 tsp onion powder
- 1 tsp garlic powder
- 1 tsp salt

In a food processor blend ingredients (about 10 minutes), or in a bowl use your hands to get it very fine. Shape into a tightly formed loaf. Place on foil-lined broiler pan. Bake for 2 hours at 300F. Allow to cool completely for best slicing into thin strips (can freeze for future use). Reheat strips gently in a frying pan just before serving. Makes 4 to 6 donairs.

TRADITIONAL SWEET SAUCE

- 1 tin sweetened condensed milk
- 2 Tbsp white vinegar
- 1 tsp to 1 Tbsp garlic powder, to taste

Mix together in a glass or metal bowl. Let stand in fridge for an hour before using (can keep in fridge for one week if you have leftovers).

Assembly

To assemble donair, gather: pita breads, thinly sliced white and/or red onion thinly sliced tomatoes, donair meat, sliced to 1/4 inch pieces, Traditional Sweet Sauce, and wax paper or foil or paper towel to wrap them up.

Reheat (and slightly brown if you like), donair meat in large skillet. Dip pita in a little water and steam in another skillet or microwave. Place pita on wax paper or foil or paper towel base. Place 2 Tbsp sauce on pita. Top with meat, chopped onions and tomatoes, and finish with more sauce if desired. Roll donair by using paper base to keep it together, and twist paper at bottom to keep things somewhat tidy. This is messy food, so have fun and enjoy it!

SHERRIE ERICKSON
Vernon, British Columbia

I developed a "something from nothing" approach to preparing meals from my mom, learning to be resourceful and creative. Even though we grew up in a large family of six kids, we always had an abundance of fresh food to eat. As a family we would go berry or cherry picking and enjoy plums and apples from our backyard in Lavington, a community near Vernon. My parents and dear family friends would purchase a pig together and have a homemade sausage making day, sharing the meat between the two families.

Like my mom, I create "something from nothing" using whatever I have on hand as well as incorporating in-season food. We purchase fruit like peaches and raspberries at local markets and family-run fruit stands. All year round we have access to local food from stores like Nature's Fare. We buy eggs and chickens from the farmer who lives across the road from us, and I grow and use my own herbs, garlic and tomatoes. I also blend my own lavender mint tea right here in my home.

I especially think to spring and summer when gardens offer fresh produce, and to the outdoor gatherings of friends and family. This is when I enjoy preparing something special like salads, my go-to for dining guests. My favorite way to present salads is on a platter – I want to create a rainbow that's gathered from the garden. What is available? Who's going to be at the table? The food has to be fresh and look beautiful; I believe if you're going to eat it, it has to look appealing. With love, I pour my heart into the dish. I love making people feel good, whether it's by teaching a yoga class or serving a meal to those dear to us.

SALAD DRESSING

- extra virgin olive oil
- apple cider vinegar
- ½ lemon, juiced

- 1 tsp Dijon mustard
- ¼ to ½ tsp maple syrup
- salt and pepper, to taste

Whisk oil, vinegar, lemon juice and mustard together. Then add maple syrup, salt and pepper. Whisk again to blend. Serve.

NICKY LARSON
Blumenort, Manitoba

We live in the town of Blumenort, just north of the city of Steinbach. The yards in this town are large, with ours being almost an acre. Our vast outdoor space is appreciated and needed for kids to play in, since we have a big family. We're a family that enjoys getting together and eating too!

While I don't mind cooking, I particularly love to bake special desserts, including a favorite that has become the tradition on birthdays: a family ice cream cake. But my go-to recipe that has been in my repertoire for at least the past 20 years or so is my no bake cheesecake.

When I first made it, it became an instant hit. Since then I'm drawn to make it because it's easy to prepare, not expensive, and can be easily doubled or even tripled for larger crowds. Besides, I do love cheesecake myself. And, if it's hot out, I do not have to turn on the oven!

It has been prepared for holiday events, significant occasions, church potlucks, and family gatherings. It's one of those versatile recipes that can be made ahead. One of my sons loves the Oreo cookie version, while my husband prefers the more traditional graham cracker one.

Whether big kid or small, this family-friendly dessert satisfies. Would you join me in a slice?

NO-BAKE CHEESECAKE

- 2 cups crushed graham crackers, approximately
- ¼ cup sugar
- ½ cup butter

- 1 package whipped topping mix (I use Dream Whip)
- ½ cup milk
- 1 cup sugar
- 1 Tbsp lemon juice
- 1 8 oz square cream cheese

To make the crust, mix together crushed graham crackers, sugar and butter and press in bottom of a pan. Set aside.

To make the filling, blend whipped topping mix and milk together. Then add sugar, lemon juice and cream cheese. Beat well until smooth. Pour over the crust and let set for about 1 hour. Garnish with your favorite fruit on top if you like.

Note: Consider using crushed Oreo cookies for the crust as well as in the filling. If you'd rather not have a crust, enjoy the filling on its own. Have fun with it and make it your own.

JOYCE DOERKSEN
Port Rowan, Ontario

I grew up in Northern Ontario; however, I moved to Hamilton to attend Teachers College and after graduation began teaching grade four. Here I belonged to a Christian youth group, and in February 1966 we all enjoyed a weekend of skiing and socializing in Owen Sound.

A group of young people from Port Rowan was also at that retreat. I met my future sister-in-law, Betty, and we started a lifelong friendship that weekend. Betty arranged a blind date for me with her brother Ed, and soon after Ed and I married. Ten years later we moved to Port Rowan, where we live today.

Port Rowan is on the north shore of Lake Erie. It's a pretty tourist town near Long Point Provincial Park. My husband's family is Mennonite. His relatives and original members of our church came to Port Rowan in 1926. Our beliefs, special dinners and celebrations are important to us and they influence the way we live our lives. I've learned to make a lot of traditional Mennonite foods, and I'm proud that I have also made foods from my English background that Ed's family enjoys.

When we get together for Christmas we have a traditional turkey dinner. One Christmas I made a special pudding that I'd enjoyed as a child. Fortunately my new family was willing to try it and today my sisters-in-law Betty and Irma consider it part of our Christmas meal. They'd be really disappointed if I didn't make Christmas pudding; they always hope there'll be some left for them to take home.

CHRISTMAS PUDDING

- 2 cups brown sugar
- 1 cup each bread crumbs, raisins, and flour
- 1 tsp each baking soda, and ground cinnamon
- ½ tsp each ground cloves, nutmeg, and salt
- 1 cup each grated apples, carrots, and potatoes
- ¾ cup margarine, softened

Combine dry ingredients together. Grate apples, carrots and potatoes. Add to dry and mix well with margarine.

Line the bottom of an angel food cake pan with waxed paper and grease well. Pour mixture into pan, cover with foil, and steam over a pot of gently boiling water for 3 hours. Check it every half hour.

When done turn out into a pie plate. Serve with warm brown sugar sauce.

ROBBIE MUELLER
Victoria, British Columbia

"This is the best steak I have ever tasted!" I gushed to the steward. It was our first "Captain's Dinner" at my husband's, Lieutenant Ernie Mueller's, new posting.

The HMCS Chaudiere was docked in 1970, awaiting orders, at the Esquimalt Naval Base located in Victoria, BC, and as is the custom, the Captain was hosting his senior officers and their wives to a dinner party when the new orders were received. Tonight's "Dine the Wives" was grand, and the orders were good. The ship would be casting off for Hawaii within the week, and that night the celebration was on.

"Thank you Ma'am, it's the steak sauce, best in the fleet! I'll tell the Chief Cook. You know it's his own secret recipe. Cookie will be pleased!" the steward replied. With that, I made it my mission to come home with the secret, and as I always get what I want, I left the ship with "mission accomplished!"

I have used this sauce for over 40 years and it's never failed to please and impress my own dinner guests. Now it's time to share with all of you, as they say in the military, on "Civi-street."

WARDROOM SECRET STEAK SAUCE

- butter – don't skimp
- 2 garlic cloves
- 2 cups ketchup
- 1 Tbsp lemon juice
- 2 Tbsp Worcestershire sauce
- 1 tsp hot mustard
- salt and pepper, to taste
- cayenne pepper (optional)

Heat a small sauce pan, melt the butter and cook chopped garlic until it's soft. Add the rest of the ingredients and simmer for at least one hour.

Want extra kick? Just add more Worcestershire sauce and some cayenne pepper.

LESLIE LEWIS
Saskatoon, Saskatchewan

We are Roughrider (football) fans out here and that means that we're Roughrider watermelon helmet heads out here too. I have a great recipe story that uses the entire watermelon, both the outer and inner parts, for game day.

Depending on the size of a person's head, a big or small watermelon can be used. I personally can fit the small one. Not sure if that's good or bad, but it is what it is!

Hope you enjoy eating the salad; have fun getting ready for the big game. GO RIDERS!

WATERMELON SALAD

- watermelon, cut into cubes or balls
- olive oil
- lime juice, freshly squeezed
- ½ to ¾ cup red onion, chopped, to taste
- salt, pepper, to taste
- feta cheese, crumbled

Cut a watermelon in half. Scoop out the watermelon flesh and cut into cubes or melon balls. Cut up a red onion. Add both to a bowl and mix.

In a small bowl, mix olive oil, fresh lime juice, salt, and pepper together to make the dressing. Pour the dressing over the watermelon and red onion. Toss gently together. Add feta cheese and stir it gently together to integrate. Place in fridge to cool and soak up the dressing.

To serve, first stir the mixture then pour into watermelon halves. When the salad is gone, feel free to put an empty watermelon half on your head, like a helmet, and you're ready for the game!

WENDY HORVATH

LaSalle, Quebec

I grew up with a father who was a chef from Slovakia. Looking back at my childhood and thinking about what we ate, it was much different than the usual chicken nuggets and hot dogs. Our meals were things like pig knuckles, blood sausages, and lots of potatoes. I still remember coming home from a day at the park and smelling the wonderful aromas that filled the house. It made my mouth water every time!

As I grew older, my love for cooking became stronger. I loved helping my dad out in the kitchen and I found it very interesting to watch how all the ingredients blended together to make these incredible dishes. Eventually, I moved out of my dad's place and married into a wonderful Salvadorian family, and that's where the fun of cooking began!

My mother-in-law showed me how to garden, since I had no idea, and every year since then I have planted a garden. I love being able to walk out into my back yard and pick a fresh cucumber or tomato to use in our dinners. One of my favorite dishes consists of all the ingredients I can grow, or the Latin Style Perogies using garden tomatoes.

LATIN STYLE PEROGIES

- 1 package frozen potato and bacon perogies
- 2 tomatoes, chopped
- ½ yellow onion, chopped
- 1 bunch cilantro, chopped
- pinch salt
- ½ lemon, juiced
- Salvadorian cream or sour cream

Fill a pot with water, add a dash of salt, and bring it to a boil. Add perogies to the water and cook them until they float to the top.

Drain perogies, then add some oil to a frying pan. Heat oil, then add perogies. Fry until each side is golden brown.

To make the tomato salsa: mix tomatoes, onions and cilantro together, then add a pinch of salt and lemon juice. Mix well.

Place perogies on a plate. Top them with the tomato salsa and Salvadorian cream. Enjoy!

ROSE HILDEBRANDT
Gruenthal, Saskatchewan

I grew up in Gruenthal, Saskatchewan, in a Mennonite family. My earliest memories of Pluma Moos (Plautdietsch or Mennonite Low German for Cold Plum Soup) would be when I was around the age of four or five. It all began a few days before Christmas, when I would watch my mom begin to cut up all the dried fruit. This chore would be a signal to me and my five siblings that Christmas was near.

As I grew older I joined in this Christmas tradition. Mom would call us girls to gather in the kitchen of the old farm house, to assist in the making of our Christmas meal. I can still remember the old two-roomed homestead, with wood burning stove, large wooden family table, and wooden bench.

After the preparation, Pluma Moos would be stored in the pantry in anticipation of Christmas morn. Following gift opening, I could already smell the aroma, which seemed to call the family to gather around the table and enjoy the sweet smooth taste of the luscious dried fruits. What a treat! Pluma Moos was truly a meal of celebration, and often enjoyed at Easter too! You can eat it warm or the way I prefer, cold.

PLUMA MOOS OR COLD PLUM SOUP

- 1 cup dried prunes, cut up
- 2 cups dried fruit, such as apricots, apples and raisins, cut up
- 4 cups plus approximately 1 to 2 Tbsp water, divided
- ½ cup sugar, to taste
- pinch of salt
- 6 Tbsp flour
- 1 tsp butter
- 1 tsp vanilla

Cut up dried prunes and place in a large pot. Add 4 cups water, sugar, and salt. Bring this mixture to boil.

Thicken the dried fruit with a mixture of flour and approximately 1 to 2 Tbsp of water, and slowly add to the boiling prune mixture. Lower the heat, and slowly cook for about 5-10 minutes. When cooked, add the butter and vanilla.

To serve, eat when warm or cold.

VIOLA LINDALA
Timmins, Ontario

I'm second-generation Finnish-Canadian, born and raised in Timmins, a gold mining town in northern Ontario, during the late 1930s.

The roast recipe that I'm sharing has travelled with us to our many homes in Toronto, Vermont and New York State. It originally comes from Karelia, a province on the southeast coast of Finland, and is a favourite throughout that country. I understand from friends from Finland that it is an everyday meal; however, to us it represents special occasions and celebrations.

Our version uses stewing cuts of beef, lamb and veal, baked slowly, and covered in a heavy cast iron roaster. This selection of meat can vary in quantity, depending on availability. After two hours cooking time the juices are slightly thickened and seasoned with salt, pepper and garlic cloves. We serve it with available vegetables on the side, complemented with sour pickles.

My godmother, who was a renowned cook at a northern lumber camp during the depression, kept men coming to work just for her food. Even there this recipe became a favourite. Because of the depression, she had to stretch her budget by thickening the gravy even more with flour.

A wide selection of our friends find this dish rather exotic and have requested it many times. If there are any leftovers they are still delicious and enjoyed heated up the next day.

KARELIAN ROAST (KARELIAN PAISTI)

- 1 lb ground beef
- 1 lb ground lamb
- ½ lb pork bacon
- whole peppercorns

Bake, uncovered, in a medium oven for 3 hrs. Serve with potatoes and red beets.

Our Version

Depending on availability (with the quantity varying as well), use stewing cuts of beef, lamb and veal, to which 3-4 ounces of water has been added, then bake slowly in a covered heavy cast iron roaster.

After it cooks for two hours, remove from the oven. Mix 2-3 Tbsp of flour with a cup of water and slowly add to the juices in the roaster. Season with salt, pepper and garlic cloves. Return the roaster back to the oven to cook for another hour.

To serve, we complement it with sour pickles and available vegetables on the side.

CARLEEN SIEBEN
Sherwood Park, Alberta

My parents have been married for 60 years, raised five kids and have prepared thousands and thousands of meals for family and friends. Through it all the RED BOWL has played an integral part of meal preparation.

You know the bowl – it was part of a set of bowls nestled inside of each other, each one a different colour. I bet your family had that set of bowls. It's only the RED BOWL left now, and it's been used for almost every meal – casseroles, Grandma's potato salad, cookies, and never to be forgotten, what my family calls Crazy Chocolate Cake with Caramel Icing.

Why Crazy Chocolate? No idea other than maybe it's crazy easy? Or maybe because once you try it, it makes you crazy that you can't stop eating it. Crazy to get up in the dead of the night and creep down to the kitchen to sneak a bite or two right from the pan, not to take a full piece mind you, just a few nibbles to tide you over. Of course, it's a bit of a stretch to explain to your kids the following morning why there are tiny fork marks along the edge of the cake. Try it and see for yourself. But I suggest you leave the stove light on to help find your way in the middle of the night – saves stubbing your toes.

CRAZY CHOCOLATE CAKE

- ½ cup butter or margarine
- 1 cup sugar
- ½ cup cocoa
- 1 egg
- 1 tsp vanilla
- ¼ tsp salt
- ½ cup milk
- 1 ½ cups flour
- 1 tsp baking powder
- ½ cup boiling water – add 1 tsp baking soda

Add all ingredients in bowl. Mix well.

Flour and grease a 9 x 12 pan, pour batter into pan, bake for 30 minutes at 350 degrees.

CARAMEL ICING

- 10 Tbsp brown sugar
- 1 Tbsp butter
- 4 Tbsp cream (or evaporated milk)
- 1 cup icing sugar
- 1 tsp vanilla

Heat brown sugar, butter, and cream to boiling point, stirring constantly to avoid burning. Remove from heat. Add icing sugar and vanilla.

Beat until spreading consistency – do not make too stiff – should be somewhat runny. Spread over cake – icing will harden.

CHERYL MILLETT
Toronto, Ontario

As a child, I consumed canned baked beans, warmed up with a chopped wiener or two, and definitely with toast and butter. I don't remember any veggies (grin). Making homemade Klondike baked beans began in my twenties, when I stumbled upon Pierre Burton's "how to" essay titled "Baked Beans," only there were no measurements (but there were veggies). It was a descriptive and entertaining way of sharing this recipe. The vision of Klondikers gnawing on frozen beans with "a locked in warmth" intrigued me. Warming any way you eat them!

Eat the beans hot out of the oven, warmed up or even cold. Serve them as the main dish with toast and butter or as a side dish if you prefer. This is a perfect potluck dish too. Create a vegetarian version, which I have done so many times. A good piece of salt pork isn't easy to find – I cannot tell you the last time I found one. This dish is delicious any way you make it.

Over the years, many people have experienced my baked beans – dined with me, sampled them, or got a mason jar full of them. I have only made them on a cold chilly fall or winter's day partly because the oven is on for several hours, but mostly because t'is the season for beans.

This one dish is a feast for all your senses: the visions of seeing the white beans turn a deep brown, the smell of awesome aromas from the herbs and more for hours on end, the taste of something so complex and delicious, and finally, yes, the sound of the sweet words of praise as it touches and warms the stomachs of your appreciative family and guests. Enjoy the warmth my friends!

KLONDIKE BAKED BEANS

- 4 small bags (450g each) navy beans
- 3 bay leaves, crushed
- 1 cup fresh parsley, chopped, less if dried
- 4 garlic cloves, crushed, divided
- 2 tsp. oregano
- 2 tsp. thyme
- 1 tsp. chili powder, to taste
- 2 tsp. whole cloves
- 2 tsp. salt
- grass-fed salt pork, ham or side bacon, optional
- 4 large tomatoes, chopped
- chili sauce/powder, to taste
- 2 tins of tomato paste (156 ml each)
- 5 medium onions, chopped (half of them chopped fine)
- 1 small bunch green onions, chopped
- 2 tsp. dry mustard
- 2 tsp. celery seed
- 2 tbsp. apple cider vinegar
- 2 bottles molasses (662 gms or 1.5 lb each)
- 1 cup sherry, optional

In a large pot, soak beans overnight in plenty of cold water as the beans will absorb a lot of water. Drain. Cover beans with fresh water. Add bay leaves, parsley, 2 crushed garlic cloves, oregano, thyme, chili powder, cloves and salt. Simmer for 1-2 hours or until the skin of the bean breaks when you gently blow on it.

Meanwhile, chop pork or bacon into very large marshmallow sized chunks (optional). Chop tomatoes and onions to have ready. When beans are cooked, drain. Reserve the liquid. Pour beans into a large roasting pan. Add pork if using.

Preheat oven to 250F. In the same large pot, pour in the reserved liquid and the rest of ingredients - except molasses and sherry. Simmer for 1 hour. Add molasses and maybe more chili powder, to taste. When the liquid is ready, pour it over the pan of beans making sure the beans are well covered.

Cover with lid and bake for a minimum of 6 hours – the longer the better. Half way through, taste them. One hour before eating, pour sherry on top if using. Bake until ready.

MAUREEN DYNNA
Shell Lake, Saskatchewan

A few days ago, a handwritten book arrived in my mailbox containing a collection of my mom's favorite recipes that she cooked for us while we were growing up. There are so many memories attached to those recipes.

We were a farming family in central Saskatchewan in the 70s when times weren't always easy, money was tight, and resources were few. We didn't go to the city for groceries very often, and our small town grocery store stocked only the basics. Our meals were simple and ordinary fare. Our city cousins felt we ate health food, and we did eat organically, before that was ever a trend. The harsh winters depleted our potato bin and we ate through jars of preserved fruit and bags of frozen vegetables, so when spring arrived we were ready for something fresh.

The first sign of spring in the garden was always the rhubarb. Never one to fear fluctuating spring temperatures, the rhubarb poked its nose through the barely thawed garden soil and flung leafy green umbrellas into the May air. Red stalks of sour goodness grew by the inch in a matter of days. While rhubarb pie was a family favorite, it took many cups of rhubarb, and we were seldom patient enough to wait for the plant to grow big enough to provide a pie's worth of rhubarb. Instead, our family tradition was to use the first cutting of rhubarb to make rhubarb fritters.

The tenderest stalks of rhubarb were diced, mixed into fritter batter, and deep fried to golden brown. Once fried, they were dipped in icing sugar and eaten hot and fresh. I think there's a good chance that some spring meals were light on salad and heavy on fritters.

RHUBARB FRITTERS

- 1 cup flour
- 2 tsp white sugar
- ½ tsp salt
- 1 egg

- ¾ cup milk
- 1 ½ tsp baking powder
- 1 cup diced rhubarb

Whisk together the egg with the milk. Mix dry ingredients in a separate bowl and then add into egg/milk mixture. Stir rhubarb in.

Drop by the spoonful into hot oil. Brown on both sides.

Remove from oil with a slotted spoon into a paper towel lined colander. Serve hot with icing sugar or white sugar.

LARISSA MAC NEIL

Inverness County, Nova Scotia

Growing up in the Maritimes on the western shores of Cape Breton, we were blessed with some of the warmest sandy beaches in Canada. As children we spent a lot of summers swimming, building sand castles, and collecting beach glass and shells. One of our favorite things to do when the tide went out was dig quohogs.

Quohogs are hard-shell clams that grow to about fist size. We would wade through the water navigating the rippled sand for tiny volcano-shaped holes the size of pennies. As the quohogs buried themselves in the sand they would spit the sand out the holes; if you dug down about 4-10 inches you could catch them. We dug them out using our feet, praying that there wasn't a razor clam or crab in the hole instead.

Often times we would have a clam boil and cook the quohogs on the beach over a bonfire. We would place a huge pot on a metal grate over the fire and load it up with the clams. We put corn, potatoes, onions, garlic and quohogs in an onion bag and boiled it in a pot of salty ocean water. Then we dumped the cooked food onto a newspaper-lined picnic table and had a big feast.

Later in the summer, when the quohogs were bigger and tougher, we took them home to cook. Mom steamed them and we shelled them, cleaned out the guts, separated the muscle from the tongue, and finally fried them in garlic butter. My mother-in-law liked to pickle the leftover quohogs for making soups and chowders later in the year. The shells didn't get wasted either. We would use the nicer ones for crafts and crush up the rest for fertilizer and feed to the chickens to strengthen their eggs.

PICKLED QUOHOGS RECIPE

- 5 lbs quohogs (hard shell clams)
- 2 cups white vinegar
- 3 bay leaves
- 1 lemon, sliced
- 1 tsp chili flakes
- 3 cloves garlic

Start by scrubbing the shells to remove any sandy bits. Steam quohogs covered in lightly salted water. Strain the liquid from steaming and place in a large saucepan. Set aside. Remove the meat from the shells. Set aside.

Put vinegar, garlic and chilies in a large saucepan with the steaming liquid, and simmer for 10 minutes. Leave to cool slightly.

Pack the cooled meat into sterilized jars, adding a bay leaf and a slice of lemon to each jar. Leave at least 1 cm space at neck of jar. Pour the cooled vinegar mixture over the meat to cover. Seal firmly and store in the refrigerator. Keeps for several weeks.

Table Talk

- When do you celebrate with food? What is the significance of the occasion?

- What is your definition of a party? Do you invite a certain number of people? What food (or drink) *must* be served?

- Have you ever celebrated alone? If yes, were you okay with being by yourself? Why? If no, why not?

- Who would you want to be at every celebratory event whether or not they still are living? How can you honour or include them somehow even if they're not with you?

- Where do you celebrate food? What location or place stirs up the feeling of gratitude for your food?

LEGACY

Legacy is a gift that we give to future generations. While food stories about tradition emphasize food events, stories about legacy emphasize the practice of handing down our traditions from generation to generation. Legacy is about our past – what we've inherited – as well as our present – what aspect of our inheritance we currently choose to nurture. Stories about legacy also encompass all of the other themes of food stories: family, life, tradition, comfort, celebration and community.

The food legacy we inherit can be richly nourishing if we recognize and honour it. Perhaps you already wear your food legacy like a well-worn mantle placed on you long ago, or a newly discovered cloak that you cherish and lovingly care for. When you actively keep your food legacy alive, it can deeply enrich your food story.

Food legacy may be passed down in many forms: in recipes; traditional, local or regional foods; special events; rituals; the events surrounding a meal, such as the activities involved in acquiring and preparing food; the meals themselves; and, of course, in food stories. When we remember special times when special food was enjoyed together, we honour our food legacy and pay tribute to loved ones who have gone before us. And when we create ancestral meals, teach in the kitchen, and *together* eat the food of our people, we keep the legacy alive so that precious dishes and customs are not lost.

CARMEN GODIN
Tracadie, New Brunswick

We have a huge tie to the area where we live. In fact, we are the first Acadians in the region, dating back to the 1700s, and have the same descendants as the Cajuns in Louisiana. Both my husband's and my family are rooted here in this French fishing community near the coast. It's not a pretty past, with the fighting between the English and the French closer to Nova Scotia – and the Acadians not willing to take sides, which almost resulted in their complete expulsion; but thanks to the Mi'kmaq heroes who kept our hiding places secret, we're here today! We're *very* grateful for our historic relationship with these great people.

In this the only legal bilingual province in Canada, we enjoy true Acadian food, like a special type of poutine – with shredded potato wrapped around pork – in large, friendly, family-oriented gatherings. I remember that as a little girl, when my dad was serving in the Navy in Halifax, our reach to home at Christmastime was through posted packages from my grandmother. It simply would not be Christmas without the macaroons she lovingly prepared and sent to our family of nine. Nobody had a lot of treats or many gifts, since nobody had a lot of money; ingredients for cookies were simply not justified unless it was for special occasions like Christmas.

We returned home to New Brunswick every summer to visit our loved ones, and moved back here a number of years ago. I now live here with my own family.

Sometimes these particular cookies may appear at big events any time during the year, but as a tradition, I make these every Christmas, just like my grandmother did so many years ago.

TRADITIONAL CHRISTMAS COOKIES

- 2 cups white sugar
- ½ cup margarine or butter
- ½ cup milk
- 6 Tbsp cocoa

- 3 cups rolled oats
- 1 cup coconut
- ½ tsp salt
- ½ tsp vanilla

Bring the sugar, butter, milk and cocoa to boil in a pot, stirring occasionally.

Mix together rolled oats, coconut flakes, salt and vanilla in a separate bowl and off heat, add to the pot. Mix all ingredients together while still hot.

Drop the macaroons onto a cookie sheet and place in fridge.

PENNY MORIN
Inuvik, Northwest Territories

I was born in Fort Nelson, BC, and moved to Edmonton, AB, when I was five years old. I come from a large family of 13, including eight biological siblings, along with adopted and foster siblings. Unfortunately, two of the 13 have already passed away.

Mom always had something ready to eat for us or for anyone who dropped in. She was a great cook, but she really loved to bake. Her lemon meringue pie, among other treats, was spectacular; but there was one thing she was really known for, and that was her bannock. She liked to experiment with flavour and ingredients, but we preferred the traditional recipe, warm, out of the oven, served with butter. I can taste it now... melted butter on each piece in my mouth!

I was almost a teenager when I moved from Edmonton to Inuvik to join my dad. Whether it was in BC, Alberta or Northwest Territories, dried meat was huge for us; but it was in Inuvik where I was introduced to caribou, muskox, dried fish, Eskimo donuts, dried whale meat, and muktuk (whale fat). These local favourites soon became part of my diet and I continue to enjoy them to this day, though I've never acquired a taste for muktuk.

From dried meat to dried fish, these dishes hold special meaning because of my strong ties to the north; but it is my mom's bannock recipe I choose to share with you. I'm glad I was able to sit with my mom before she passed, to write down ingredients and measurements for her recipe. I hope you enjoy it as much as I do!

MOM'S BANNOCK

- 4 cups flour
- ½ tsp salt
- 2 Tbsp baking powder
- 1 Tbsp sugar (optional)
- 1 ½ cups warm water
- 2 Tbsp melted lard or oil

Mix together dry ingredients. Set aside. Mix warm water with lard or oil in a separate bowl. Mix liquids with the dry ingredients. The less you work with bannock, the better.

Bake at 450F for ½ hour. You can bake in a slab or in muffin tins. If you use muffin tins, this makes 12.

SUE TROMBLEY
Terrace, British Columbia

I received "the cookbook" as a Christmas present. It had a white plastic coil binding, lemon yellow paper for the front and back covers, and pink pages to indicate food divisions. It had blank pages on the reverse side of the recipes, so I decided to use the cookbook as my recipe file, collecting favorite recipes, including my Mum's.

My Mum grew up with lots of kitchen experience and many recipes memorized. Every Saturday my Mum would make bread, cookies, cakes, pies and biscuits. She passed these recipes on to me, and I then passed them on to my own children. They took turns working in the kitchen with me, progressing from cookies and cakes to roast beef and Yorkshire pudding, roast turkey and stuffing, lasagna, pastry and bread-making! My son, Réjean, received accolades from a friend when he ate some rhubarb pie Réjean made. My son, Brent, thought that everyone grew up with the same home cooking education and had confidence to prepare meals and read recipes. My daughter, Jodi, became a Red Seal and Journeyman Chef.

Many years later, the cookbook has aged as I have. It no longer has its yellow page covers, half the coils from the white plastic binding are broken off, some of the pages are loose and the ones still attached to the binding all have darkened and frayed edges. It is in a reserved part of my cookbook shelf, off to one side to hopefully prevent further damage. My children have families of their own and have asked for favourite recipes from this book, which are easy to spot because they have been splattered with ingredients that left a testament to the goodness of the recipe. The difficulty is choosing just one of those recipes to share with everyone, but my final choice is the much loved Lemon Loaf.

LEMON LOAF

- 1 cup of sugar
- ½ cup shortening
- 2 eggs
- ½ cup milk
- 1 ½ cup flour
- 1 tsp baking powder
- ½ tsp salt
- grated rind of 1 small to medium sized lemon

Cream sugar and shortening, beat in eggs one at a time, then lemon rind. Add dry ingredients alternately with milk.

Bake 350F in oven for 1 hour. When cool, top with ½ cup white sugar and juice of 1 lemon.

ELEANOR SCHULTZ
Halifax, Nova Scotia

This is a tribute written about Eleanor Schultz and her special Blueberry Grunt recipe, by Natasha Tremblay, her granddaughter.

This recipe was my grandmother's, and unfortunately she is no longer with us. Thankfully what our family does have to remember her by are a few of her special recipes. Perhaps in the same magical way a song can take us back in time and help us relive moments from our past, aromas and tastes can do the same.

When I think about my grandmother I always see her sitting at her kitchen table. It was her spot. I also very much like to be in the kitchen and sit at my table too.

In my opinion, following a recipe that holds memories does well for the heart and soul. I believe it does just that for my mother whenever she decides to make this dessert. She also gave me her blessing to share this sacred family recipe in hopes that others enjoy it as much as we have.

BLUEBERRY GRUNT

- 3/4 cup blueberries
- 1 cup sugar
- 1 Tbsp room temp shortening
- 1 Tbsp room temp butter
- ¼ cup sugar
- 1 egg
- 1 cup milk
- freshly grated orange rind (optional)
- 2 cups flour
- 2 Tbsp baking powder
- ½ tsp salt

Preheat oven to 350F.

Spread blueberries evenly at bottom of casserole dish. Pour 1 cup sugar over them.

In a small bowl mix shortening, butter, sugar. Add milk, egg and orange rind.

In a separate bowl mix flour, baking powder and salt. Add wet mixture to dry, making a smooth dough.

Scoop heaping spoonfuls over the blueberries (about 3 rows of 3 scoops). Bake for 30 minutes or until browned.

Let cool 15 minutes before serving with vanilla ice cream or whipped cream.

JENNIFER CUMMINGS
St. John's, Newfoundland and Labrador

While Salmon River Chicken might not be a traditional Newfoundland recipe, it is one that comes to mind when I think of home. I grew up in outport Newfoundland in the amalgamated communities of Centreville, Wareham, Trinity and neighboring Indian Bay. These four towns formed a tight-knit community where everyone knew each other; friends were family and family were friends.

Growing up in Newfoundland we knew one thing: the weather could be miserable! Cold and windy winters, the seemingly ever-present rain, drizzle and fog in the fall and spring and even periods in the summer. Weather like that brings comfort food, the kind of meal that warms you on those miserable days. For me, Salmon River Chicken was one of those. The smell in my Nan's house when she made it? Amazing!

It is a Newfoundland twist on fried chicken; the key is savoury. Dried savoury is a staple in every Newfoundlander's pantry. I swear it makes everything taste better, including this chicken! Salmon River Chicken, despite the name, has nothing to do with salmon or fish at all!

The chicken was a town favourite at a small family-owned diner in the 1980s. It was located in Indian Bay right next to Indian Bay River, one of the best places for Salmon fishing in Newfoundland. Thus the name became Salmon River Chicken. The diner didn't have the best of luck; it suffered a small fire in the mid-80s, and was rebuilt only to suffer a devastating fire in 1988. The family did not rebuild again, but Salmon River Chicken lived on and families in the communities started perfecting the recipe at home. Now nearly 30 years later it has been handwritten in my own recipe book for my family in St. John's.

SALMON RIVER CHICKEN

- 6 to 8 chicken legs (or any bone-in chicken parts)
- 2 eggs
- ½ cup of flour
- pinch of salt & pepper
- 1/3 cup savoury – can substitute thyme, marjoram, or sage if you cannot find savoury
- ½ cup milk
- 2 cups of breadcrumbs

Pre-boil the chicken.

For the batter mixture: beat eggs then stir them into the flour. Add salt and pepper. Add a little of the savoury into this mixture. Add milk and stir. Pour batter mixture into a deep dish. Mix remaining savoury with breadcrumbs in another deep dish. Cover chicken in batter mixture and then dredge in the breadcrumb mixture.

Cooking methods have varied. Many use a deep fryer to get the golden brown crunchy batter on the chicken. Others without a fryer have used a frying pan with oil to brown. And still others, who are trying to avoid the extra fat, have cooked the chicken in the oven at 375. Personally I like the perfect crunch from the deep fryer. I like my comfort food with a little extra indulgence on the side!

KAREN ALTON
Manitou, Manitoba

It's just a little black book 6 ¾" x 4 ½". The cover is falling apart and pieces are flaking off. The writing inside is faded and in different colours of ink. It is my Grandmother Walker's Recipe Book.

To me it is full of stories. It speaks of a time and a community now gone, the community of Appleby in Halton County, Ontario. The time could be the 1930s.

Each recipe has a name with it – friends, relatives, neighbours. Some of these neighbours and friends were to be my future relatives. There are pictures of a number of the people in the book too.

The first recipe in the book is a Fruit Cake and it has my great-grandmother's name with it. The last in the book is Pancakes and it came from Modern Priscilla (a magazine). Grandmother had set up an index inside the back cover and there are three extra additions: Chocolate Sauce, Butterscotch Pie and Hand Lotion (!). There is also a recipe for School Fair Cookies 1916. Hmmm, maybe someone had a sweet tooth.

SCHOOL FAIR COOKIES 1916

- ½ cup white sugar
- ½ cup lard
- 1 egg
- pinch of salt

- ¼ cup sweet milk
- ½ tsp baking soda
- 1 tsp cream of tartar
- flour to stiffen

That is all it says. Modern recipes would tell you just how to combine the ingredients and if you needed to roll the dough out or drop from a spoon onto a cookie sheet.

In 1916 you would have been using a wood stove, too, and know just how hot the oven had to be for cookies. There was an art to knowing the temperature by just sticking your hand into the oven. Apparently it was decided by how long you could hold your hand in there comfortably.

It makes me remember the old way of measuring – many ladies used an old teacup, quite often minus the handle. That was the standard 1 cup measure. Cookies would be cut out by using a glass or a baking powder tin. Things have certainly changed.

WALLY PATCH
Fraser Lake, Wentworth, Quebec

In loving memory of my dad, as captured by words spoken by him, and added to by me, Deborah Hutchings, his daughter. Note: I created a pamphlet for him using the words below even before we knew he was sick and passed. I'm so glad I crafted it, and now I get to share one of his well-known and all-time favorite recipes with you. His words:

I've been named "Mr. Fiddlehead" by those who know me since I've been picking and bottling fiddleheads for many years. These plants have been growing on my land – in the ditches. It has come to be known as Lost River Fiddlehead Farm. It's not really a farm in the field sense but in marshy and wet areas that they thrive around property.

I enjoy providing both fresh and pickled fiddleheads to my friends. Fiddleheads also freeze extremely well. What do they taste like? They have an interesting taste that I would say is halfway between asparagus and spinach. I not only enjoy pickling and eating these delicacies but I get to spend time in the bush with lots of beautiful wildlife. Come and join me!

FAMOUS FIDDLEHEAD PICKLES

Blanche fiddleheads for 4 minutes. Drain and repeat. In a large pot boil the following for 5 minutes:

- 1 tsp tarragon
- 1 tsp celery seed
- 1 tsp salt

- 2 Tbsp sugar
- ½ cup water
- 1 ½ cups white vinegar

Place drained fiddleheads in sterilized jars. Add hot liquid and seal. Process in a hot water bath. I hope that you enjoy!

NIKKI STADNYK
Rolling Hills, Alberta

When I grew up there were always fresh homemade pickles on the table with every meal. Mom would cut them up lengthwise and put them in a crystal dish. There were seven hungry kids to feed so most of the time it was our appetizer. They rarely made it to the table!

Mom, Margaret Skuban, made these pickles from scratch every year. The pickles were always tangy, with just the right amount of dill and garlic, and no matter how long they were preserved that year the jar always opened with a pop and the pickles still had a crunch.

Pickling day was always a huge process. Mom never did anything small, not with seven kids to feed. But there was lots of help and everyone had a role in the process. Baby cucumbers needed to be picked from the garden or gathered from other sources. Then the jars and lids needed to be washed (a quick run through the dishwasher worked great). Then the prickles, dirt and sometimes leftover cucumber flowers had to be washed off. The next step was stuffing the jars full of cucumbers. And as an added bonus mom would sometimes add baby carrots to the jars, my favorite.

A few months before my mom passed away at the age of 86 I got to make pickles with her one last time. I cherished every moment as we stuffed baby cucumbers, dill and garlic into the jars. She made sure I followed the brine recipe exactly, so they would turn out the same as always. I loved the sight of them all lined up on the counter and the sound of the pop as they sealed. The original 1958 recipe has been passed onto me and I will honour the tradition in years to come.

MARGARET SKUBAN'S PICKLES

The following mixture is for 1 quart jar:

- ½ cup white vinegar
- 1 tsp sugar
- 2 tsp coarse salt

- 1-3 spray dill
- 3 cloves garlic

Scrub cucumbers and pack them in clean jars.

Pour mixture over cucumbers and add cold water to fill the jar. Seal and store in a cool dry place. (Sealing is boiling the jars in a hot water bath.)

Allow 4 - 6 weeks to cure.

JOHN HUTCHINGS
Stephenville, Newfoundland and Labrador

I grew up in a large loving family. Our extended family was no different; my mom's family was large and loving as well as my dad's. My uncles were all fishermen and loved salmon fishing. While we enjoyed lots of salmon and other fish, we also ate wild game like moose meat, wild bird and chicken. Fish cakes would often be served during mealtimes as well. Our gardens produced abundant crops to warrant pickling and canning to ensure we could enjoy the bounty throughout the winter. The food was wholesome, the produce fresh, and everything was made from scratch. We felt mom's loving touch in every meal. She ensured that there was plenty of food to feed eight daughters and four sons.

We looked forward to festive holiday meals like Christmas, when we ate anything from moose to salmon steaks to rabbit. But Sunday dinners were especially the highlight of the week. Everybody showed up for this food celebration after church. Often when it was a fine weather day, we would pack up and head to the river. These picnics on the river bank became a tradition; there was nothing better than eating outside, beside the water, and meeting up with our friends and other family members. The food was precooked or semi-cooked and finished on an open fire as necessary. Baked chicken or ham typically became the staple meat on these occasions, along with plenty of vegetables and other tasty delights. Often after the meal, the boys fished, the girls picked wild berries, and Mom tended a garden they had at the river.

We are thankful that our mom cared and fed our large family like she did. We were hard working folks; our bellies were always full, thanks to mom. Family gatherings were important to us then, and now have been passed down to our children as a food legacy.

POACHED SALMON

- 1 whole salmon
- 1 onion, chopped
- 3 celery stocks
- lots of carrots to feed family
- 2 bay leaves
- 4 Tbsp vinegar
- squeeze of lemon

Place the salmon in big pot. Add enough cold water to cover the fish (it must be covered). Add the onion, celery, carrots, bay leaves, vinegar a generous amount of salt and pepper.

Cover with a lid or tin foil and bring to boil on the stove. Once boiling, turn off the heat and allow the fish to stand in the water until cool. Carefully remove the salmon, place onto a board, scrape off the skin and place on a large flat serving dish. Finish with a squeeze of lemon.

Note: Salmon, with the ends cut, would be frozen in a block of ice in the summer in a 2 liter milk carton to enjoy in the winter when times were tough.

SUSAN TAYLOR-GOL
Toronto, Ontario

When I was a child, I spent summers with my grandmother, or "Mummu," in Helsinki, the beautiful Finnish capital on the shores of the Baltic Sea. We spent a lot of time together at the outdoor central market place, or "kauppatori," where she would poke fresh salmon on display. Mummu would pick one and have the salesman fillet the salmon by removing all the bones, leaving a slab of pink fish with skin attached. It would be wrapped up in wax paper and we would carry it home in a shopping bag.

Once home, Mummu would pat dry the unwrapped salmon and sprinkle it generously with coarse salt and sugar. She would then chop fresh dill and cover the slab with the green dill hairs. It would then be rewrapped tightly in the wax paper and placed in the refrigerator to cure for at least 8 hours.

Later in the night, when everyone else was asleep, my grandmother and I would meet in the kitchen and be the first ones to sample the freshly cured salmon. This was called our late night snack, or "iltapala," and she would take her special knife and slice thin pieces of salmon and place them on a slice of heavily buttered black rye bread. I was her golden child, or "lapsi kulta." We would eat fish and talk late into the night about her life. I cherish these memories.

To this day I love the taste of freshly cured salmon. When my children were younger, I often purchased fresh salmon and showed them how to prepare it the same way their great-grandmother prepared it so many years ago. The key to this recipe is to use exceptionally good quality salmon, which in Canada is not hard to find.

FINNISH GRAVLAX OR GRAAVATTU LOHI

- slab of fresh salmon
- several teaspoons of coarse salt
- several teaspoons of sugar
- one large bunch of chopped fresh dill

Wrap seasoned salmon in wax paper and allow to cure in the refrigerator for at least 8 hours. Must be consumed within 3 days.

MARY BUDGELL
Halifax, Nova Scotia

Memories are such a gift. There are so many little things that make me think of my dad, but nothing tops that list quite like the smell of bread baking in the oven.

As a child, kneading bread was so much better than playing with play-dough. My father showed me how to coat my hands with flour so the dough wouldn't stick. He taught me how to press and stretch the dough with the heel of my hand before folding it over and repeating the pattern until the consistency was just right. Helping my dad make bread was a special kitchen experience. Making cookies was fun, messy and fast. Baking bread was cathartic, thoughtful and slow.

My dad's decision to make bread for our family of six instead of buying it didn't always make sense to me. It was so much work. With time, I realized that what my father had really taught me was the importance of delayed gratification. His values live in every loaf. As a child, I envied my friends' cheese whiz sandwiches on crustless white bread with juice boxes and fruit roll-ups. I see that envy in my own children now as they eye the convenience foods that line the grocery aisles and question why they too can't have wonder bread.

I guess it's time to roll up my sleeves. It's my turn to teach the importance of delayed gratification, by showing them that with a little flour, yeast and patience you can learn a lot more than just how to make a delicious loaf of bread.

POPPA'S WHOLE WHEAT BREAD

- 1 cup milk powder
- ½ cup brown sugar
- ½ cup shortening
- 2 Tbsp salt
- 1 cup seeds (red river cereal, flax, sunflower)

- 4 cups hot tap water
- 1 tsp white sugar
- 1 cup warm water
- 2 Tbsp dry active yeast
- 6 cups wheat flour
- 6+ cups white flour

Place brown sugar, salt, milk powder, shortening and seeds in large bowl. Pour in hot water. Stir to melt shortening. In small bowl stir white sugar into warm water. Sprinkle yeast into bowl. Let sit 10 minutes. When yeast has dissolved, stir, add to large bowl. Use whisk to combine. Shortening should be melted. Add 2 cups wheat flour. Whisk until smooth. Stir in 2 more cups. Add last 2 cups, stirring well.

Begin adding white flour. Around the third cup, use hands to push and rotate dough as more flour is added. When dough doesn't stick to hands, remove onto a work surface. Sprinkle flour on surface and dough. Press down on dough using the palms of hands. Fold. Rotate dough 90 degrees. Repeat. Continue adding flour whenever dough is sticking to hands or surface. When it stops sticking, keep kneading for about 10 minutes.

Shape dough into a large, fairly smooth mound. Place in large oil-greased bowl. Twist dough to cover with oil. Invert bowl on work surface, covering dough to let rise (up to 2 hours).

After dough has risen, sprinkle flour on a clean work surface. Put dough on top. Shape into long sausage. Cut into 4 pieces. Sprinkle more flour on surface. Shape each piece into a sausage by folding edges towards middle, pinching edges together. Repeat, until when you flip over pinched loaf, top of loaf is smooth.

Place each loaf in a pan. Cover. Let rise for 45-60 minutes. Just before hour is up, set oven to 400F. Oven rack should be placed at level above lowest level. Remove cover. With a sharp knife make 3-4 slits on top of bread. Bake for 30-32 minutes. Let bread rest on wire racks for 30 minutes before slicing.

KIMBERLY STRIEMER
Castlemore, Ontario

Growing up in a family of six on a 100-acre farm north of Toronto in the 1960s, we didn't have much in the way of luxuries. In fact, the century-old brick farmhouse we were living in didn't even have a bathroom until the early '60s, but the small kitchen occasionally had a special treat welcoming those who entered it.

You see, neighbours were kind in the small farm community, and one time when we were visiting Mrs. Hunter next door in her small wooden shack, the delicious smell of a loaf wafted out to greet us. Before we left, my Mom had written the recipe down.

I don't know how long Mrs. Hunter had the recipe before we finally came by it, but years later when I was old enough to learn how to bake, this loaf was one of the first things that I can remember making (not that it lasted long with so many waiting for its warm moist flavour to be pulled out of the oven)!

I even remember one day in particular, when we had to quickly make a second batch of them and have them driven 1/2 an hour away to the town where my Mom was selling them at the Saturday morning Farmer's Market, because they'd sold out so early.

Our farm and the community has been paved over and replaced by subdivisions, but Mrs. Hunter's memory lives on through her recipe, smelling just as tantalizing as it did when I first learned to make it back in that old farmhouse kitchen. And she'd be well pleased, because she always loved to share and would pass anything on that she could.

MRS. HUNTER'S BANANA BREAD

- ½ cup butter or margarine
- 1 cup white sugar
- 2 eggs, well beaten
- 3-4 bananas, mashed
- 4 Tbsp sour milk
- 1 tsp vanilla extract
- 2 cups white flour
- 1 tsp baking soda
- 2 tsp baking powder
- dash of salt
- walnuts, to taste

To make the wet mixture, in a bowl, blend together well the butter or margarine, sugar, eggs, bananas, sour milk, and vanilla. Set aside.

To make the dry mixture, in another bowl, mix flour, baking soda, baking powder, salt, and walnuts.

Add wet mixture to dry and stir just until moist (don't over mix).

Bake at 350F in a greased loaf pan for 45-50 minutes until a tooth pick comes out clean. For muffins, bake for 18-25 minutes.

This moist and delicious old favourite is good any way, but it's especially delicious with butter spread on it when it is fresh right out of the pan!

MICHELLE COLLINS
St. John's, Newfoundland and Labrador

Growing up in Newfoundland, whenever people stopped by the house for a cup of tea, there was always food involved. My mom loved to cook, but she wouldn't always have baked goods in the house. It wasn't her favorite thing to do, and we got used to not having sweet things. So whenever Mom would bake caramel squares I knew that something special was going to happen.

I always asked, "Who is coming over," or "Where are these going?" She would always act "offended" and then tell me that so-and-so was going to be coming by, or that she was going to an event. It became a running joke between us. She would cut out the squares and leave the edges that touched the pan, as they were a little crisper that the gooey center pieces. Those were the pieces that we could eat.

Many years ago, I got a "Personal Cookbook" at my wedding shower, a book that I could use to collect my own recipes. The first one I entered was Mom's recipe for caramel squares. It is still the most used recipe in that book, and every time I make it I think of her. It has been eight years since she passed away, and I miss her every day. I am grateful for all the things she taught me, and that I can pass this recipe and a little bit of her story along to you.

MOM'S CARAMEL SQUARES

- 1 cup brown sugar
- ½ cup butter
- 1 egg (plus 1 egg yolk)
- 1 tsp baking powder
- 1 ½ cups flour
- 1 tsp vanilla
- 1 egg white
- 1 cup chopped walnuts
- 1 cup brown sugar

Cream butter and sugar. Add egg and egg yolk, and vanilla. Mix in flour. Press the base into 8x8 pan. Set aside.

Beat the egg white until soft peaks form, then fold in walnuts and brown sugar to make the topping. Pour over the top of the base.

Bake in 350 F oven for 35 minutes. The topping will stay "gooey" even when baked. Cut into squares to serve.

CALVIN KRUGER
Edmonton, Alberta

My family grew up on venison. Everyone from my grandfather down to my brother and I, and now our wives, have had venison on their plate as an integral part of their lives.

But venison isn't something that is easily acquired; real hard work has to be put in to obtain it. It's never just about what is on the plate – it's the process of harvesting, cleaning, butchering, packaging, storing, cooking, and then finally eating. We performed these processes together, as a family, and the memories are what makes this meal special.

I remember hunting, my grandfather, my father, my brother and I, out in a field in November, walking on the ridge of a coulee. The snow was up to the tops of our boots and we could see our breath as we walked. The silence was always deafening. Suddenly, branches break in the coulee below, and out walks a young buck, no doubt roused by our footsteps. The shot rings out, the deer falls, everything is silent once more, and the process begins.

"Mom, what's for dinner?" I ask. "Deer, späetzle, some red cabbage. Want to help?" All at once, my memory of the hunt and the work that followed come flooding back. "Yeah," I say, underplaying my excitement. Mom taught me what she knew that evening and over many more evenings before she passed on.

I now cook for my family using my mother's most important ingredient – love – and her knife, which was gifted to me by my father. Every meal I make is a tribute to my mom, my teacher, and to memories of cold November mornings and warm evenings in the kitchen. May this story be a fitting remembrance and an inspiration to see beyond what is on your plate.

VENISON STEAKS

- 2 venison steaks (inside round, loin, tenderloin, or otherwise), trimmed
- 1 L buttermilk (or 1 L whole milk plus ½ lemon, juiced)
- sea salt, to taste
- 1 tsp black pepper
- ½ tsp cumin
- ¼ tsp coriander
- 2 cloves garlic, minced
- ¼ large red onion, minced
- 1 Tbsp vegetable oil

Marinade steaks in buttermilk/whole milk and lemon juice mixture for at least 24 hours. (This is the most important step as it tenderizes the meat and is the trick to removing the gaminess.) After marinade time, rinse milk off steak and pat dry.

Combine minced onion, minced garlic, vegetable oil, salt, pepper, cumin, and coriander in a small bowl. Cover steaks with this mixture and seal in a Ziploc bag for approximately one hour.

Preheat barbeque to high. Remove steaks from bag, grill for 4 minutes, flip, and grill for 3 minutes. Cook to medium rare. Remove steaks from grill and let rest for 10 minutes.

Serve with garlic mashed potatoes and Brussels sprouts sautéed with garlic and onion, deglazed with chicken stock until reduced.

Serves 2.

Table Talk

- What food tradition has been handed down to you from a previous generation? Do you practice this food tradition? Why or why not?

- Who has influenced you from the past to cook an ancestral or traditional meal? What is the significance of this food?

- What food practice or tradition pays tribute to or shows respect for your ancestors? How often do you honour this tradition? When and where is the food practice performed?

- What food helps you to feel closer to a loved one who has passed on? When does food help you to remember special people who are no longer with you?

- What would you like to leave as a food legacy to future generations (recipe, ritual, preparation technique, etc.)? Who can benefit from receiving this food legacy?

- What will you do to keep your food legacy alive so that precious dishes and customs are not lost?

CONCLUSION

As you read this book you probably experienced moments when someone's story about food triggered your own poignant memories, or when you felt you knew exactly what the storyteller was saying. This is because the indelible memories we have about food are most often connected to the themes of our lives that we all have in common: celebration, legacy, comfort, community, culture, family, tradition, and the transitions and transformations of life. In this respect, we all share a common food story.

The stories in this book also remind us not only of the central place of food in all of our lives but also of the way food and memories related to food shape our sense of who we are. Food and the stories we tell about food help define our nation, our culture, our families, and ourselves. When we tell our food stories we pay tribute to our shared identity as well as our individual identity.

Unique You

While the food stories in this book reveal our common food story, they also demonstrate the fact that we are all different and have our own unique food stories to tell. This may seem obvious, until you think about why there are so many generic off-the-shelf or one-size-fits-all packages and plans out there that dictate how and what people should eat. These prescriptive products may put people into a kind of food prison, where they feel they are not allowed to express their own individual stories and pay tribute to their unique past.

Because you are unique, you can *celebrate your individuality* and distinct experiences, memories, and tastes. You can relish in the fact that there is only one of you, and celebrate the food you love, even if it's not considered "healthy" by some. You have valuable knowledge to share that nobody else has and an important food story to express. Honour your unique story, acknowledge its value, and share the wisdom you have learned so that you can nourish yourself and those around you.

When I chatted with my identical twin sister Lana about some of what we considered as our most memorable food experiences while growing up, it may come as a surprise to you that not one of our food stories are exactly the same. As youngsters we were together at almost every table and gathering and pretty much ate the same meals. But that doesn't mean we recall the same memories or remember things the same way. While we love many of the same kinds of food, we have very different food stories – just like everyone else!

The story that follows is a small piece of my sister's larger food story. While Lana and I were always together visiting our grandparents at the same time, I actually don't remember some parts of the story she tells. The experience she recalls obviously made an impact on her and is now part of her own unique food story.

What follows my sister's story is my larger food story, which is an acknowledgement of the themes of this book and a way to tie it all together.

I then conclude this chapter with a brief anecdote and a cherished recipe because they represent my food journey and show how exploring just one aspect of your food story can be a jumping off point for discovering, developing, and expressing your larger food story.

LANA OLSEN
Vernon, British Columbia

You know fresh produce is important when most of your backyard is dedicated to growing it. This was the case for Baba and Dido, my Ukrainian grandparents, who lived in Vernon. Each summer our family would venture to Vernon to enjoy quality time with Baba and Dido and the wonderful activities the Okanagan region offered.

One particular fond food memory is about a meal I made when I was around 13 years old. It was likely a Sunday evening – while my grandparents were relaxing, watching the evening news – when I was encouraged to compose my own lunch type of meal, since earlier we would have indulged in a larger dinner after church. I remember how exciting it was to have the freedom to choose whatever I wanted for my salad, with items such as Baba's fresh garden produce along with local cheese and ham sausage.

During the week we'd spend hours at Kalamalka Lake. Almost always we'd have a picnic lunch filled with something fresh from Baba's garden that seemed to taste better with beach sand in it! After a day at the beach, we'd be treated to a main meal and a glorious dessert, such as fresh raspberries and cream. There was no such thing as ugly discarded fruit or vegetables, as everything was used. No food waste was allowed!

Vernon was not the only place I ate garden-fresh food. When I was growing up we had a large acreage garden where clearly my grandparent's passion for gardening rubbed off on my mom (their daughter). Now, even though I live in a desert where it is difficult to grow garden produce, I am always grateful for my past because it has guided me to continually place value on locally-sourced organic food.

My Food Story

When I think about my food memories I realize that I have many that take me back to my childhood. My mom often liked to create meal plans and experiment when cooking. More often than not, our everyday meal usually consisted of a meat of some kind, a vegetable, a starch – primarily potatoes, because my dad loved them – and a side salad that typically included iceberg lettuce pieces, sliced tomatoes, and chunks of cucumbers tossed with a store-bought dressing.

It was a treat to go out to eat or get takeout. If we did go out, it was usually to a buffet restaurant on Mother's Day. I also recall times spent in the car at a drive-in, sipping on root beer and happily consuming a burger. It made me feel so grownup. My sister and I could get our dad's mouth drooling by talking about tasty chicken on our way home from church. If there wasn't already a roast in the oven my dad would often succumb to our pleas for takeout, and then we'd fight over who got to cradle the hot bucket of chicken on her lap to inhale the aroma all the way home. Ah, yes, chicken and I go way back in my food story. It definitely continues to be an important part of my story now.

When my mom made traditional Ukrainian food, like varenyky, holubtsi or nalysnky, we counted ourselves very fortunate. I can remember having contests to see who'd eat the most varenyky and then suffering silently afterwards due to overeating. But they were so good, especially with onions fried in butter and a pile of sour cream on top! I would often boast to my friends about what I ate and was proud to talk about my cultural heritage.

I helped tend to our large gardens on the acreage by weeding, harvesting vegetables and fruit, and more weeding! Fall signaled it was time to take in the last of the crops, primarily root vegetables and tomatoes. It was hard work, but it was made fun by my dad's playfulness in the greenhouse and garden patch, especially when we were uprooting potatoes. I get sentimental when I think about these precious childhood times with my father, who passed away in 1999.

I'm sure when I was old enough I was asked to help cook, but those memories for some reason are a bit fuzzy. On the other hand, we were always permitted to help with baking, and Christmas was *the* occasion to go all out, and I mean all out! I can remember the excitement of planning with my mom what we were going to bake. She was the master of the entire process, from organizing the ingredients, to rolling or cutting cookie dough, to assembling squares. I learned a lot from her! It was normal to have at least a couple dozen varieties of goodies on hand in the freezer. This abundance was our holiday tradition.

Some other food memories include the inevitable clean-up after a meal, and the piles of pots, pans, dishes, serving trays and cutlery that fell upon mainly me and my sister to wash. Now I realize this was actually a positive bonding time with my sister, all while we scrubbed the dishes. Despite the spats, the nit-picking – "you missed a spot" – and the incident when the knife just barely missed stabbing my toe, I recall our time and chats with fondness. We were nourishing our relationship from an early age, even when doing chores after we ate.

At age 21 I was introduced to some tremendous flavours when my sister, our friends and I traveled through Europe. My food knowledge increased as I learned about the dishes that were beyond my familiar family, community and culture. It left me hungry to discover more about foods from the countries we visited as well as dishes from around the world. This trip launched my interest in global cuisine.

My Ukrainian roots meshed with German heritage when I married into my husband's family. Larger family gatherings meant traditional German dishes prepared by my husband's mom. I happily consumed this new and delicious food and welcomed it into my food story. I have now collected a few recipes from my mom-in-law and have been challenged to replicate them at home.

When we were just a couple, I didn't feel entirely responsible for providing food in the same way I did after our children were born. When it was just the two of us, I knew that my husband could fend for himself. But unfortunately, after we had kids, I became anxious about food. Making meals was something I dreaded and feared. I expressed it like this in Dianna Lee Bowes's book, *Fabulous@50 Re-Experience*:

> In my early married life it was easy to please our tribe of two with simple dishes. Things shifted when our family expanded to three, then four…
>
> I wish I could say that family meal time in our household was a delightful picture of happy people taking time to savour food while enjoying each other's company. (145)

The expectations I placed on myself to be *the* best cook for our family had me lose my grip on reality and my identity. I forgot that I was still me, with wisdom to make decisions about food and making meals. I desperately sought approval at the table and became overwhelmed with the expectations I placed on myself to ensure our family would "eat well." I discarded my food knowledge under this self-imposed pressure. Clearly I was derailed, and I projected that pain at mealtimes.

Several breakthroughs later, thankfully, I learned how to relax about cooking and my ability to provide sustenance. I also recognized the importance of how we ate and with whom, of setting the tone and focusing on more than what was on our plate. My understanding of complete nourishment was growing.

My lifelong interest in food and nutrition culminated after graduating with a diploma in natural nutrition. I opened my own business. I sprouted! In this new venture (and adventure) I continued to add to my food story by developing recipes for individual and corporate clients, leading local food challenges, creating and facilitating workshops, and teaching food and nutrition courses.

During this time, I began to see certain nutrition themes pop up during weight-loss counselling or as I discussed meal planning ideas and nutritional recommendations with my clients. It was because of those conversations that I created the *Your Food Story* program for both individuals and groups. It was a thrill to connect food storytellers with one another in meetings and hear stories develop during individual sessions as well. I witnessed significant breakthroughs in the way people saw food and their own food story. There was a definite need to share these stories.

Writing this book was an experience that demanded I further explore my own food story. When I began this book project, I couldn't imagine how I would be affected. Who knew? As I curated, read and wrote, I constantly found myself reliving moments in my life when there was food present. I was taken back to church suppers, family events, our annual Kozak family reunions, potlucks at work, girls' night out, anniversary and birthday parties, work bees where I sat side-by-side with Ukrainian elders making traditional foods, and so many other times that were formative to my food story.

Let's actively look for opportunities to tell food stories. When and where will you share your food stories? Where can you go to be with storytellers? How can you connect to and within your food story community?

I hope that my last anecdote on the next page, along with all of the food stories in this book, will inspire you to tell *Your Canadian Food Story*.

LORETTA KOZAK FRIEDRICH
Edmonton, Alberta

Borscht is a dish that honours my Ukrainian food legacy. I'm not too sure when I first tasted it – perhaps it was as a very small child living in Toronto; but I definitely enjoyed it while growing up on our acreage near Spruce Grove or visiting our Vernon grandparents. As children, we devoured our Baba's green borscht (with sorrel, known as Shchavel in Ukrainian) or yellow borscht (with sauerkraut), but it was the red beet borscht that was the most familiar then and that I now prepare the most.

This must-make seasonal soup represents my love of fresh and earthy tasting garden produce and the fulfilling effort to grow them. I prefer the good old-fashioned technique of hand cutting the ingredients. I suppose it's because I feel closer to the food that way and don't mind wearing the badge of colorful stains on my hands afterwards. Besides the red beets, carrots, onions, peas and green beans shine in supporting roles; but it's the potatoes that make me feel close to my late father, who absolutely relished eating them. The vegetables and dill have to be fresh from my garden or purchased from a farmer's market in our community. It must be locally sourced for the best taste! I eagerly look forward to the soup's aroma, beckoning me to partake of this nutritious ruby dish.

For our family, this has always been a pleasing and very tasty dish. Don't forget to add more sprigs of fresh dill (except for my husband!) and dollops of full-fat sour cream on top!

LORETTA'S BORSCHT

- 9 cups chicken broth
- 2 cups beef broth
- 1 heaping cup diced onions
- 4 cups beets, sliced in long, thin finger-like pieces
- ½ cup peas
- 1 ½ cup green beans
- ¾ cup carrots, sliced
- 1 ½ cups cabbage, chopped in small chunks
- 1 ½ cups potatoes, cubed
- large handful fresh dill, finely chopped
- 1 Tbsp raw honey
- ¼ to 1/3 cup white vinegar, to taste
- sour cream, to taste

Add vegetable ingredients together with the broth in a large pot and simmer for about an hour, stirring occasionally. Then stir in the dill (reserve some for garnish if desired) and simmer for another ½ hour, stirring occasionally.

After vegetables have softened somewhat, add the honey and vinegar. Simmer for another hour or so to really combine the flavors. Serve with sour cream and dill on top.

NOW WHAT?

Discover Your Food Story

Chapter Themes

You can begin to discover your own powerful and unique food story by exploring one of the themes of this book: community, comfort, family, life, tradition, legacy, culture, community. When you read through this book, what chapter theme triggered especially stirring food memories? Maybe you were reminded about the importance of food traditions and are now motivated to create or reintroduce a tradition. Perhaps strengthening ties to community or learning more about cultural food is now a priority. Identifying a theme that is particularly meaningful to you is a significant first step towards discovering your food story. Focusing on a particular theme will also help you uncover other themes in your food story that you would like to develop and nourish.

"Table Talk" Revelations

The "Table Talk" questions were designed to invite you to pause after each chapter and recall food memories related to the chapter's theme, spot food memories that captured your attention, and focus on specific food memories you are curious to explore further. When you reveal food memories, they can help you decipher the connection between past experiences and what you now choose to eat. Powerful food memories reveal truths and provide the direction and clarity needed to unfold your food story.

The chapter questions are examples of what you can ask when you are either alone or with a group of people. Responding to these questions will prompt food memories, help you understand their meanings, and foster conversations that support the development of food stories. Both individual reflection time and group discussions are powerful methods to discover your food story.

Senses

It is amazing how senses get time-stamped in memory. How, for example, smell can arouse a nostalgic feeling, and taste can transport us back to a moment in time. The details that are locked in your food memories may include how the food was presented, where you were eating, and the faces of the people you were with. Exploring sensory memory can release the food story within.

Consider:
- sight (pleasurable plating, unforgettable views)
- smell (poignant fragrances and aromas)
- taste (outstanding flavours, distinct temperatures)
- touch (interesting textures)
- sound (overwhelming silence, exciting clatter)

Releasing notable senses from your food memories can also be particularly powerful in helping you identify what senses are important to you, and how, when and where to use them to enrich your food story.

Develop Your Food Story

Research

To cultivate your own food story, consider doing research on what food is available and eaten in our country. You may want to study about another culture in Canada, or focus on specific foods produced in a certain region or procured in a particular locality. Read books, articles and blog posts, listen to podcasts and attend food talks to appreciate food variety in your community. Learning about meal-preparing practices, food preferences and eating behaviour in Canada will increase your food vocabulary, expand your food knowledge, and develop your awareness and connection with Canadian food culture.

Ask Questions

I encourage you to be curious and ask questions as a way to advance your food story: Where does our food come from? Who are the people who grow or produce our food? What are the handling or processing practices? While I recognize that there can be real limits to what food we can acquire (due to locality, seasonal, and pricing restrictions), perhaps we *can* find ways to support our local food suppliers. Consider foraging in the wild, taking a cooking class, growing a garden, and participating in food-related work bees. No matter whether in-person or online, you can set up times to meet with a hunter-gatherer, gardener or meal-maker and record noteworthy recipes and relevant stories. Efforts to be with other people to ask about their food choices and stories will benefit your own food story development.

Cook or Bake

Another way you could develop your food story is by cooking or baking. Perhaps when you read one of the 110 recipes in this collection a certain recipe intrigued you. Making a new dish will increase your food knowledge, even if you're a veteran cook or baker. You may even want to infuse your own style in a recipe. If you can, recreate a meal from your region or ancestors to develop your cultural food story. Whatever recipe you use to practice your skills, whether testing a recipe by yourself or with a group of people, you can enhance your food experience.

Express Your Food Story

Share Meals

Share a meal to express your food story in a practical way. I challenge you to go beyond your accustomed group and invite those from outside of your usual community, culture or friendship circle to dine with you. Consider working alongside dining guests to create the meal together; ask thought-provoking questions about food traditions or cultural dishes that relate to the meal when eating; and encourage conversation while "breaking bread" to truly nourish everyone at the table. In this act of hospitality you are expressing your food story and enabling others to share their own food experiences as well.

Tell Stories

Besides partaking of meals and engaging in food conversations together, there are other ways to express your food story. For example, you can capture food pictures with an accompanying anecdote and relay them on social media, write a blog post, host food storytelling groups, or create collaborative events with other storytellers. Perhaps you should be the next speaker at your local food conference, to share excerpts from your food story on a larger stage. (Why not?!) You have a food story. We need to hear it!

Join Our Community

A welcoming place where we can discover, develop and express our food stories is in the *Your Food Story* community. There is room for everyone to be a member of this group. Consider this as my invitation to you to join me and others at the table. What's #urfoodstory?

For more exciting information and current updates about this or other related projects visit urfoodstory.com.

ACKNOWLEDGEMENTS

I wish to express my sincere thanks again to all of you contributors for relaying precious stories with me that collectively became a food and recipe storybook. You are all family to me now.

To the farmers, gardeners, foodies, food bloggers, chefs, restaurant owners, and other food industry leaders, particularly from my surrounding food community – I think of you, your food, and your love of eating, producing, processing, picking, creating, cooking, and/or serving. Thank you for making a huge impact on my food story!

To my reviewers, Michele Genest, Barb Rees, Sylvia Cloutier, Dana VanVeller, Lindsay Anderson, Myriam Porrazzo, Wendy Gibson, and Christal Sczebel – I appreciate the time you each took to carefully read and then capture into words the message of this book. Your outstanding reviews validated my efforts. My heart is full.

Dorothy Briggs – you have no idea how much you motivated me to complete this book! Sincere appreciation for all that you do.

Sandy Miller – my food story was developed because of your life story group. Very grateful, dear friend, for your wisdom.

Jean Paré – cook and baker extraordinaire. Cookbook queen. I'm your biggest fan! I'll always remember that you opened your door to me. Many thanks for your feedback on this book too.

Teresa Spinelli – your food legacy lives because of your dedication! Thank you for your inspiration. I'm so grateful to have you in my life.

Dianna Bowes – your generosity, creativity, and support is deeply appreciated, my fellow food-lover and sister. You are the truest friend.

Tina Kruger – can you see, amazing cook and baker, and dearest sister, I did it?! I feel your hugs from heaven. In my heart, always.

Diane Strelau – you always stimulate my senses, nourishing me with your culinary creativity! I cherish you and our sisterhood.

To my Kozak and Pinchuk kinfolk, especially my mom (Mary Pinchuk in this book), grandmothers, and aunts – thank you for your ever-lasting influence on my food story. I am very blessed.

Lana – can we get any closer? Our bond strengthens through it all. Now, let's go get a treat! Love you, my twin.

Emily and Laura – I get teary-eyed (no surprise, right?) thinking about your love and support. This book is for you. Always love, mama.

No words can adequately express my gratitude, Martin, for all you have done for me, especially on this project. How you listened to my heart and captured the vision with me, and then when writing, coaxed the words out of me to express them when I at first couldn't. Your exceptional talent as a professional editor and writer has no limits; your gift as my husband is priceless. No matter what path lies ahead, I'll continue to walk with you every step of the way. I love you.

Thank you God for the food.

CONTRIBUTORS INDEX

RECIPE INDEX

Loretta Friedrich is a food lover, educator, speaker, writer, author, recipe developer, and award-winning business owner. She is certified in holistic nutrition and has appeared in numerous magazines and on local TV. Loretta enjoys seeing canola fields in bloom, gardening, getting vegetable stains on her hands, and the smell of humus-rich soil! You'll often find her chatting with farmers and producers at local markets.

To connect with Loretta:

@sproutnatural   @sproutnatural   @sprout_urfoodstory   lorettafriedrich
                        @urfoodstory

sproutnaturalnutrition.com
urfoodstory.com